Powerless to Powerful

Powerless to Powerful

Leadership for School Change

Charles Salina, Suzann Girtz, and Joanie Eppinga

ROWMAN & LITTLEFIELD
Lanham • Boulder • New York • London

Published by Rowman & Littlefield
A wholly owned subsidiary of The Rowman & Littlefield Publishing Group, Inc.
4501 Forbes Boulevard, Suite 200, Lanham, Maryland 20706
www.rowman.com

Unit A, Whitacre Mews, 26-34 Stannary Street, London SE11 4AB

British Library Cataloguing in Publication Information Available

Library of Congress Cataloging-in-Publication Data

ISBN 978-1-4758-2234-2 (hardcopy)
ISBN 978-1-4758-2235-9 (paperback)
ISBN 978-1-4758-2236-6 (ebook)

∞™ The paper used in this publication meets the minimum requirements of American National Standard for Information Sciences—Permanence of Paper for Printed Library Materials, ANSI/NISO Z39.48-1992.

Printed in the United States of America

To the community of Sunnyside, Washington; the staff at Sunnyside High School; and the leadership of the district office. These mission-driven folk truly are our inspiration. To the students at Sunnyside, whose courageous behavior transformed a community.

And to Sonya, for her endless patience.

Contents

Foreword

Rick Cole, Superintendent, Sunnyside Schools

The book you are about to read, and the knowledge and strategies you will gain from it, is a complete game changer in the realm of public education. How can I say that with such conviction? As the superintendent of Sunnyside School District, I had a global view of the improvement process that one of the authors of this book, Dr. Chuck Salina, led as the turnaround principal of Sunnyside High School. I had a front row seat as he applied the academic theory you will read about to action with a clear and uncompromised vision for student and staff success. This led to an amazing story of success for our high school, school district, and entire community.

Sunnyside High School was considered a perenially low-achieving school by state education officials, an almost constant fixture on the state's lowest 5 percent list with a graduation rate hovering around 50 percent. This changed quickly when Dr. Salina agreed to take on the challenge of leading the turnaround effort at the school. He was given the freedom to implement the dramatic, and sometimes uncomfortable, reforms and initiatives you will learn about throughout this book. This may have seemed like a gamble to some, but not to me. I had known Dr. Salina for a very long time. I knew he had the knowledge, character, and leadership skills to accomplish the daunting challenge he was tasked with. He did not disappoint. He successfully developed and implemented a school system on a foundation of relational trust, academic rigor, and social support.

The results were nothing short of amazing. The culture change at the school was palpable. The change in belief that students and staff had in themselves and each other was incredible. They were no longer maligning themselves into believing that success was impossible or that believing in themselves was hopeless. They developed a strong, forward-thinking philosophy that stated their futures would not be determined by the circumstances they were faced with in the present. They were no longer fighting against one another, trying to gain power and control over something that was powerless and uncontrollable. They were now working together and pushing each other to improve and succeed; they were owning their destiny. They became a family, and "together we will" was their mantra.

Because of the strategies you will soon read about in this book and the leadership and commitment of its author, Sunnyside High School is no longer seen as one of the state's lowest-performing schools. In fact, it is now celebrated as one of the state's highest-achieving schools. The graduation rate has risen to 85 percent and continues to rise. We are also closing the achievement gap at a lightning pace. Out of 295 school districts in Washington, Sunnyside High School has the highest graduation rate for transitional bilingual students, the fourth-highest graduation rate for special education students, and the eleventh-highest graduation rate for students who come from poverty.

The results we experienced were remarkable, but also completely replicable. The driving principles and conceptual framework that Chuck Salina, Suzann Girtz, and Joanie Eppinga lay out in this book can be applied to any school system. They have proven beyond effective in the most difficult of circumstances. However, these teachings cannot be cherry-picked; they must be wholly adopted. Like a three-legged stool, the principles and practices of relational trust, academic rigor, and social support will not be effective in the absence of one or another. I hope you enjoy this book and embrace the hope it can bring to sometimes hopeless situations. It worked for us; I know it can work for you.

Preface

In the fall of 2008, Sunnyside High School District had just closed down its alternative high school site. The district's leadership wanted to bring all high school students under one roof, believing that the new configuration would promote equity of resources for all students. Typically, alternative programs designed for at-risk students face several problems, including:

- Difficulties in recruiting new teachers (NCES, 1996);
- Staff who are less experienced (NCES, 1996);
- Higher staff absenteeism (NCES, 1996);
- Fewer teachers who are qualified in the content area (Ingersoll, 2004); and
- Reduced likelihood of meeting state educational targets (Johnson & Ward, 1998).

Sunnyside's alternative school was no different; it faced many of these problems.

The district's leadership team members felt a strong sense of ownership regarding this new program implementation, meaning they wanted to do the right thing by their profession and by their consciences. They wanted to serve each of their students and believed strongly that the alternative-school students would receive a better education at the comprehensive high school.

The alternative school had a dismal success rate: Less than 42 percent of the students were graduating.

SUNNYSIDE'S STORY

Sunnyside High School (SHS) was not a typical middle-class suburban high school. SHS, with more than 1,700 students, historically had a graduation rate hovering around 50 percent. The high school had been consistently identified by the Office of Public Instruction in Washington State as a low-performing school, in the bottom 5 percent of all comprehensive high schools in the state.

All but 5 percent of students were eligible for free or reduced lunch; 87 percent had minority status; and 14.5 percent were designated as ELL (English Language Learner) students. The average income in the community was $35,000, and gang problems were a significant issue. Many students' parents worked as migrant farm laborers and had two or three jobs.

A deeper examination of what was working and what was not at the school included a review of what was known as the *intervention program*. The intervention program, unlike the alternative school, was located on the campus of the high school and was designed for students who had high failure rates in their course work, were non-special education, and had poor attendance.

Three professors from Gonzaga University, which had entered into a friendly mentoring relationship with the high school, examined this program. They found that the program was graduating 80–90 percent of its students, which was significantly higher than the graduation rate at either the alternative school or the regular high school. The question became apparent: *What were teachers and students doing differently in the intervention program that resulted in such a high graduation rate?*

During the next school year, 2009–10, Sunnyside applied for the federally funded School Improvement Grant. One of the requirements of the grant was that the district would have to choose one of four options:

- Turnaround model: replace the principal, and rehire no more than 50 percent of staff;
- Restart model: convert the school, or close and reopen it under a charter school operator;
- School closure: close the school building and enroll the students who attend that school in other schools in the district that are higher achieving; or
- Transformation model: remove the principal and take steps to increase teacher and school leader effectiveness; institute comprehensive instructional reforms; increase learning time and create community-oriented schools; and provide flexible and sustained support.

An external review, required as part of the grant process, observed that the district had the greatest potential to positively impact student achievement by following the transformational model. The district was awarded the federal Title 1 grant in April of 2010. The district had approximately $1.5 million per year for three years to help improve the graduation rate at the high school.

The district applied for—and received—a School Improvement Grant (SIG), which meant they could hire a turnaround principal. An advantage of SIGs is that they allow people to think creatively. They reduce the importance of external thresholds and give leaders the breathing room to figure out where and how to shine the spotlight that will result in positive change.

When the turnaround principal arrived at Sunnyside, he found that the teachers and the support staff were discouraged, students had lost their focus, and administrators were busy putting out fires. Staff were working hard going through the motions of doing school, but evidence of learning was hard to find.

As the conversation deepened with staff and the leadership team, themes emerged reflecting a lack of trust and a sense of hopelessness. Finger-pointing was rampant—"If only students would . . ." "Administrators should . . ." and "Teachers need to . . ."

GETTING HELP

In seeking candidates for the position of "Transformational Principal," the district created a job description and interview questions based on the Chicago Public Education guide—*School Turn Around Competencies*—that emphasized a specific skill set unique to a turnaround leader. These competencies, as defined by Steiner, Ayscue Hassel, and Hassel (2008), included the ability to identify and achieve "quick wins," a willingness to break organization norms and rules to achieve goals, and the ability to move quickly from ideas to action (p. 5).

The new principal was granted significant operating flexibility and freedom to go after quick wins. The flip side of that autonomy was that the pressure was on to produce results. The question the turnaround principal asked himself was: *How do you empower people to do the work differently?*

LEARNING ABOUT SUNNYSIDE

The turnaround principal faced immediate challenges. Before school had even begun, a teacher informed him, using decisive language, that the principal could not make the teacher be involved in a specific training that was part of a district-wide initiative, which the teacher considered to be worthless. The tension in the air was high as staff watched the new principal's response closely.

After moving the conversation to his office, the principal suggested that they start over, introducing himself and asking the man's name. He then suggested that the two have a civil conversation and that the teacher refrain from telling the principal what he was or was not going to do.

The men had an earnest conversation. The principal listened as the teacher outlined his concerns. He then told the teacher that he would investigate the effectiveness of the training, but that meanwhile it was required; nonetheless, he was sure the two could find common space from which to operate.

Later that day, staff brought up concerns in an open-microphone setting. They asked the principal what he was going to do about the problems in the school, which were defined as a failure of the administration, parents, and students to live up to agreed-upon expectations.

Teachers reported that administrators were not acting on attendance and discipline issues and did not support teachers on the tough issues with students and parents. Teacher after teacher commented that if the kids were *at school* and would *obey the rules*, they would be able to *teach them*; but without a strong commitment from the administration, their efforts were a waste of time.

The perception was that kids ran the school, that they did not want to learn, and that, without support from the administration to ensure that students toed the line, no learning would take place.

The teachers clearly felt unsupported, and they were pushing back on the students because of it. Teachers were angry, frustrated, and tired of being told that they were ineffective. They felt as powerless as the students, yet their perception was that they were taking the brunt of the criticism for failure. As people tend to do, they were pointing blaming fingers elsewhere, including at each other. In spite of all this, many staff did comment on their willingness to improve and acknowledged that positive change was possible.

The principal held numerous one-on-one and small-group conversations with students before school began. The kids were as candid as the teachers in describing where the problem lay and why the graduation rate was so low. Several students expressed their strong belief that some staff didn't care about their success.

Most interesting was that the majority of students expressed the sentiment that the problem at the school rested in themselves, explaining that many of the "students just don't care about school—it isn't for them" and that many had too many barriers in their lives to meet the demands of the graduation requirements.

Yet students expressed a strong desire to graduate. They seemed to be resigned to the notion that they were the reason for the school's failure, and they felt powerless to do anything about it. What was also surprising was that the students were not fully aware of the scope of the problem: that more than half the students were *not graduating*. Upon hearing that result, one student said to the principal, "After all, mister . . . this is Sunnyside. What do you expect?"

To learn whether this attitude was common, the principal held an open forum for parents and learned that, indeed, this perception of themselves as second-class citizens was prevalent. Uncharacteristically, more than 100 parents came to meet the new principal. The primary concern expressed by parents had to do with the quality and delivery of the school lunches!

When the principal asked the parents about graduation rates, it became apparent that, although they cared, they felt inadequate to express their concerns and intimidated about advocating for their children in the academic realm. Some talked about teachers' lack of caring, or counselors and administrators not communicating. But it became clear that they *wanted* to believe in their school. Like the staff, they were well-intentioned people who had a strong desire to see the students succeed.

Finally, the principal met with consultants, some of whom had been working with the school for the previous two years under a special district-wide state improvement grant. Despite the trainings offered by the consultants, the number of students who were failing was growing. The principal realized that the essential resources for creating school change were already in the building, and that with appropriate support, teachers, counselors, and administrators could raise student achievement without outside help.

The principal then asked the leadership team for data regarding the number of juniors and seniors who were on track to graduate. After a long pause, the leadership team assured the principal, "We have everything under control." A call to the counseling department produced the same (delayed) response.

Two days later, the numbers came in from the counselors: Of the approximately 400 seniors still enrolled, only 75 were on track to graduate, and the number of juniors who were on track was 73 out of 364.

USING THE DATA

The administrative team then dug deeper into the data to analyze where students were on their journeys toward graduation. The data revealed that at any given time in the previous year, less than 60 percent of the students were passing all of their classes, and less than 25 percent of the senior students were on track to graduate. Student tardies were out of control, and the number of suspensions was unacceptably high.

Gains in graduation had been made (the rate in 2009 was 49.7 percent, and in 2010 it was 64.8 percent), but many staff and administration believed that was because corners were being cut through easy online credits retrieval programs. In some cases, students were making up full course requirements in less than a day. Furthermore, specific requirements were being waived by administration.

Marginal students who did graduate did so with an undue amount of assistance from highly dedicated staff, but there were no real schoolwide systems to support teachers and students over a long period. Many of the staff believed that the graduation number was not representative of students who had actually earned their diplomas. One teacher observed that during the previous year's graduation ceremony, she had counted student after student who'd had a credit waived by administration for one reason or another to ensure the student graduated. The teacher asked, "Why should I care if a student learns in my class if the administration only worries about the graduation number?"

BEGINNING THE CHANGE

At the assembly held on the first day of school, curiosity was high: Who was this person who had extended the school day for an hour four days a week; delayed after-school co-curricular activities for an hour once a week so that all teachers, including advisors and coaches, could work in teams to improve curriculum and assessment processes; closed campus for freshman and sophomores; insisted that juniors and seniors had to earn the privilege of leaving campus for lunch; and instituted mandatory noon-time study hall for all students receiving less than a C+ in all of their classes?

The principal's first words were, "Would every other student in the gym please stand up?" He then told those standing up to leave the gym, "because you will not graduate." The gym was silent as the students looked at the number of students standing. Nobody moved.

Then the principal told them to sit down. He explained that historically less than half of the school's students had graduated and that this was not going to be the case this year. Then he asked all the staff to come to the center of the floor. Over 100 strong, they stood before their students and made a pledge that they were all committed to helping each other do *their own* work: helping the students graduate.

Staff made a commitment to not allow any student to fail. The principal explained to students that the new programs and policies had been put in place to help them, not punish them. All of these programs and other processes that were being implemented (which will be discussed later in the book) were intended to improve graduation rates. An almost palpable sense of both hopefulness and fear arose from those in the room. The principal assured them that together, they *would* improve the graduation rate. And indeed they did—from 49 percent to 84 percent in four years.

SKIN IN THE GAME

Before that happened, though, the established pattern was that everyone looked to someone else to fix the problem. The major stakeholders believed that the graduation rates could be fixed if *others* were more willing to step up.

- The staff had not lost their sense of mission, but they were not feeing supported or heard in doing their work.
- Parents wanted to believe in their school, but they did not know how to navigate the system and blamed the school for not communicating with them.
- Students wanted to graduate, but many believed they did not have the capacity to do so or were too far behind.

Everyone needed someone to show them what to do and how to do it.

The turnaround principal notion sometimes seems as if it is grounded in the old way of thinking of heroic leadership, but as Heifetz (1998) explained, leadership means influencing the community to face its problems. So, who owns the problem? Heifetz's answer would be: *everyone who is a member of the system, including students.* One of the primary challenges for the new principal would be to figure out how to get everyone in the school to own the problem—how to get everyone to have "skin in the game."

The challenges, successes, and strategies employed at Sunnyside do not stand alone. Schools throughout the nation are struggling to raise student achievement in the face of ever-increasing external pressures. This book was written to provide leaders with a road map for making that struggle productive, enriching, and humane. It was written to remind leaders: Power is making people feel as if they have choices.

Acknowledgments

We admire the scholarly thinking of Stephen Covey, Thomas Sergiovanni, Robert K. Greenleaf, and Carl Glickman. The profundity of their words didn't become apparent until their ideas were taken back to the schools and applied there—at which point it became apparent that these authors were offering a powerful new way of doing business.

We also recognize the contributions of Dr. Richard Cole, the superintendent of Sunnyside School District, and the school board at Sunnyside; Gonzaga University, especially Dr. Jon Sunderland, for its willingness to take risks and allow a unique partnership with Sunnyside; graduate students from the Gonzaga–Sunnyside cohort, who drove us to engage in deep thinking about social support, academic press, and relational trust; and the administrative leadership team at Sunnyside High School, who were willing to be pushed beyond normal human limits in their endless hours of service to others.

Finally, we want to acknowledge all who are willing to engage in the conversation about transforming schools.

Introduction

Sharing the Lessons

This book shares lessons learned from a college professor–high school principal lens, telling the story of schools in which courageous students, educational staff, and communities take on the enormous challenge of improving graduation rates, student achievement, and school-wide morale. It offers a *new way of thinking and leading* that results in a different way of doing business.

The book comprises two parts, described in summary below:

Part I—The Framework. Part I delineates the conceptual framework and the related principles necessary to implement a vision of achieving a graduation rate of 100 percent. Having a clear framework that drives systems in the change process is critical in the process of making decisions that are intentional rather than haphazard.

    This framework is anchored by the theories of academic press (high expectations), social support (helping others achieve desired outcomes), and relational trust (depending on others). Throughout, the framework is suffused with the systemic notions of servant-leadership.

Part II—Lessons Learned. In Part II, the role of leadership (with and without authority) and lessons learned in transforming schools that feel powerless are discussed. The format is this: Try something; reflect on it; adjust according to the feedback.

    The Lessons Learned describe mistakes made and triumphs achieved as schools move, on a consistent, ongoing basis, from the status quo to a new ideal. These eight chapters describe the behaviors and beliefs required to reconnect all stakeholders to the vision and mission through a systems approach—a necessity for leaders in a low-performing school.

Part I

Driving Principles and the Conceptual Framework

Today's teachers are so busy trying to keep up with and implement state and federal mandates that they have very little time for reading, reflecting, sense-making, and applying research-driven practices. Consequently, administrators often hear, "Just give me what works and the steps to implement it so I can go back to the real work." This frantic pace is also dismaying for formal leaders in our schools. How often do formal leaders move staff forward based on the latest idea or program that will solve the most immediate crisis in the school, without developing a deep understanding of the underlying principles? Burnout is not an issue when people are deeply embedded in mission-driven work. Burnout occurs when people are frantically pursuing activities that seem to them to be unrelated to improving teaching, leading, and learning.

This activity-driven approach to change that is so prevalent in our schools is like the story of a man who is busy climbing a ladder that's leaning against a wall. When he finally gets to the top of the ladder and peers over the wall, he realizes he was busy climbing the wrong wall. It is essential to have an overarching plan before beginning the climb. The plan should be grounded in driving principles and the core purpose of our schools—student learning.

Covey (1992) prompted leaders to define what their *true north* is so that they are able to self-correct when the going gets tough. Importantly, this orientation encourages leaders to make decisions that are grounded in principles rather than decisions that are random and situation based.

A conceptual framework helps to describe an overarching plan or concept so that an intentional approach is used to guide the work in a specific

1

direction. It refers to the structure of the mental approach, or, as Shields and Rangarajan (2013) define it, the "way ideas are organized to achieve a research project's purpose" (p. 24).

Schools are living laboratories in which lines of inquiry are actively followed daily to improve learning. If a leader isn't working from a conceptual framework, especially in a school where people feel powerless, these lines of inquiry or problem solving are random at best and may actually be doing harm—not only within the classroom, but also to relationships between people.

SUPPORTING PRINCIPLES

Before giving a description of the conceptual framework that drives the change process at a low-achieving school, this book offers the principles that support its development. The primary principle is this: If we are to contribute to the greater good, we must ourselves be nurtured and nurturing in all realms of existence.

The notion of pursuit of the greater good lends itself to serious discernment and a call for action. Knowing what is best may not always be easy or obvious. Leaders may have to use their ethical discernment, which is related to working through difficult problems and putting core values into action (Covey, 1989).

An ethical education is dedicated not only to developing the whole person, but also to challenging each person to contribute to society by tending to the common good and a sense of social justice that is focused on the poor, the vulnerable, and the marginalized. Robert Greenleaf (1970) offered principles that each of us can manifest in helping others be their best selves and then contribute to the well-being of society. His model, known as *servant-leadership*, is grounded in providing others with a sense of belonging through working to their higher-order needs and building their capacity. Then they in turn become servant-leaders whose actions are grounded in social justice.

Many of today's education agendas evidence the principle described above. However, discerning what is best and how leaders should work toward the greater good is difficult, and confusion may arise as leaders move toward specific actions that support the common good. Currently, such issues as equity and access to quality teaching and learning for all students raise serious questions to which there appear to be no easy answers.

If educational leaders are to move forward on difficult issues, they must have a conceptual framework driven by core beliefs. Reflective practitioners without a framework upon which to base their decisions are much like a ship lost in a storm. What are they reflecting upon if they are not grounded in anything?

At that point, reflection devolves simply into one individual's best thinking—a ship sailing without a rudder. A ship must have a rudder if it is to move with intentionality. However, if the rudder is too rigid, the ship can't adjust to the vagaries of the sea. The conceptual framework and guiding principles must allow the practitioner to be adaptive to address difficult problems, because in reality there is no real final solution—only *continuous improvement toward a continually redefined ideal.*

Many of today's educational policies are an attempt to address our current social justice issues and what is best for the whole person. For example, the No Child Left Behind Act was intended to help our most marginalized students be identified and then, ideally, better served. The desire to close the achievement gap, along with the belief that each student could succeed at high levels, spoke not only to a sense of social justice, but also to the notion that educating the whole child is a focus on the common good.

Yet efforts toward promoting the well-being of each child came at great expense to the people who did the work. The environment in schools that feel powerless is often toxic and nonhumanistic; it fails to reflect a belief in the worth and dignity of those who are doing the work. A fear-based approach, supported by consequences such as charters and firings of principals and half of the staff, was promoted at the state and federal levels, as well as by the business sector, for schools that were failing.

These are misguided actions that are not embedded in intentional, integrated principles. Each of these is a very narrow approach to change and transformation that actually results in harm. Servant-leadership is grounded in the notion that people will be successful if the right support systems are present and capacity building takes place.

Just as educators must embrace the notion that each student can be successful, it is equally important—if not more so—that a formal leader truly believe that his or her staff can do the work.

THE CONCEPTUAL FRAMEWORK

The conceptual framework described in the next few pages applies to *both the adults and the students* in the school. The framework consists of the concepts of academic press, social support, and relational trust, presented via the principles found in the theory of servant-leadership, which emphasizes humanism and social justice.

The thinking behind the framework emphasizes the importance of liberating people so that each will achieve his or her fullest potential. How these concepts play out may be different depending on the specific context, but the driving principles and the related framework are the same. After the conceptual framework is described, specific understandings and practices are presented in Part II.

Academic Press

Academic press emphasizes high expectations, accountability, and academic rigor (Lee, Smith, Perry, & Smylie, 1999, p. 5) for *everyone* in the school. Although academic press is only one of the cornerstones of the model for change, much of the work in schools centers on this facet, and readers will recognize it in phrases such as *power standards, essential learnings, Common Core,* and more.

Focusing solely on this one lever for change is actually counterproductive. Beliefs and behaviors about capacity for academic press are given short shrift because the primary spotlight is on the *activities* of academic press, which consist of the pressures within the school environment to meet academic goals and standards (Shouse, 1995) and includes the extent to which *students and staff feel pressure to achieve academic success* (Lee et al., 1999).

This pressure to achieve academic success comes at many levels—not only from adults to students, but also adults to adults, students to students, and, yes—even students to adults. Academic press can offer a framework and a vision, providing both students and teachers with the opportunity and the motivation to achieve at higher levels.

In discussing high academic standards, researchers (Natriello & McDill, 1986; Ormberg, 2013) reported that effort and achievement, as indicated by grade point average, increased when standards were raised. Students want to succeed, and they appreciate it when the adults in their lives hold high expectations for them. At the same time, they're sometimes uncertain about whether they can meet those standards.

Academic Rigor

A major contributor to academic press in a school is academic rigor. As Quint, Thompson, and Bald (2008) noted, "Delivering a demanding yet accessible curriculum that engenders critical-thinking skills as well as content knowledge" creates academic press (p. 38).

But access to a rigorous and well-articulated curriculum is missing in many of today's high schools and is almost nonexistent in a school that feels powerless. Poorly performing high schools often have lower standards that are not aligned and find creative ways to allow students to achieve minimal state graduation requirements.

According to a report published jointly by the National Center for Public Policy and Higher Education and the Southern Regional Education Board (2010), almost 60 percent of students who graduate from high school in the United States are not prepared for postsecondary studies and must take remedial courses.

Consequently, political pressure increases regarding such non-solutions as high-stakes testing, and more recently through the Common Core, that attempt to align curriculum nationwide with common assessments, in efforts to ensure that students are ready for the next grade level, course, and graduation. This was one means of developing a sense of equity for post–high school expectations.

Student-to-Teacher Pressure

Academic press in which pressure is applied at all levels of the system is powerful in the *first steps* of initiating change and improving performance. One of the most interesting points of academic press in schools where this framework is applied is the way in which students put pressure on teachers to improve.

- When students realize that their grades influence whether the campus will be open and determine certain other privileges, they put pressure on teachers to enter grades on a more regular basis to better reflect their progress in a timely manner.
- When meeting standards becomes an emphasis, students are more willing to receive help from their peers or teachers.
- When simple data systems are put in place that keep track of how many students are passing each class, teachers more frequently remind students of course expectations and provide additional avenues to allow students to improve their grades.

Teachers and students in these circumstances remind each other of the expectations to improve their chances for success. They also increase two-way communication that focuses on accountability and improved learning.

There is no doubt that a well-articulated curriculum that is rigorous, aligned with standards, clearly defined regarding what a student needs to be able to know and do, and supported by common assessments is essential to ensure that academic press is present within a given school. Selecting high standards and facilitating adherence to those standards is one of the most potent means by which positive change can be made in a low-achieving school (Quint et al., 2008).

In the context of staff attending to issues of curriculum, DuFour (2004) made the following points about maximizing academic press via engagement at the teacher level:

1. The best-designed curriculum has no impact unless it is taught (implemented vs. intended).
2. The likelihood of implementation increases exponentially if teachers feel ownership of the curriculum.
3. Ownership is directly related to engagement.
4. The greatest engagement, and thus the greatest *ownership and loyalty*, takes place in the smallest part of the organization to which people belong. ("Assumptions Regarding Curriculum")

Unfortunately, schools that feel powerless are experiencing curricular chaos (Schmoker, 2006). The implementation of the Common Core *by itself* does not ensure ownership and loyalty at the classroom or building level—even if the resulting curriculum is of high quality.

As DuFour et al. (2004) observed, when group ownership and understanding of the curriculum are lacking, especially in a low-performing school, limited academic press will be present at both the adult and the student levels. Extensive *external* professional development won't ensure successful implementation. It takes teams of teachers working together to make sense of a curriculum before it can be applied equitably with all students, according to DuFour et al.

Newmann and Wehlage (1995) pointed out:

> The most successful schools are those that use restructuring to help them function as "professional communities." They find ways to channel staff and student efforts toward a clear, commonly shared purpose for student learning. They create opportunities for teachers to collaborate and help one another. Teachers in these schools take collective—not just individual—responsibility for student learning, and for constantly improving their teaching practices. ("Organizational Capacity")

Performance Mastery

Performance mastery is Bandura's (1977) term for achieving significant goals. Teams of teachers successfully implementing a new curriculum driven by high standards and resulting in higher levels of student learning would be a form of performance mastery. Research (Stein & Wang, 1988) shows that self-efficacy scores assigned by teachers increase when innovative programs are implemented successfully.

Believing in Each Other

When staff work in isolation at low-performing schools, often the result is that staff are pitted against staff and/or against administration. Staff working in a troubled school often have lost sight of the mission of the school and, more importantly, don't believe that the school as a whole is capable of helping each student be successful.

Academic press implies that *all* stakeholders have a common understanding of academic standards (Lee et al., 1999). Furthermore, the staff must communicate to the students that each of them is able to reach these standards. After academic press was applied at one school that had previously suffered from low scores and low morale, students and teachers made the following comments:

- "It shows us that we can do it."
- "This year is better than last. . . . [Academic press] is keeping everyone on their toes. Everyone wants to come to school."
- "Making folks earn it motivates them to come."
- "If you raise standards really high they can be met. I didn't think that before."
- "AP Chemistry is a month ahead of where it was last year. I get more finished in class; I have less homework."

Students and teachers at the school had an increased sense that students were academically capable.

The most effective way to build capacity in others is to demonstrate the belief, in both *words and actions,* that they will succeed at a very high level, and then support them in doing so. After student input was solicited at one low-achieving school, a new expectation was put forth: An average daily attendance of 93 percent would be necessary for juniors and seniors to gain off-campus privileges during lunch.

For the first six weeks of school, the two classes consistently came in well below the mark. In the seventh week, they nearly reached it—92.5 percent. The leadership team discussed whether the score should be rounded up to encourage the students and let them have off-campus privileges. The conversation centered on how hard the students had been working and administrators' belief that the students *deserved* those privileges.

As a group, the leaders came very close to giving in—until a colleague reminded them that the students had *not* earned their privilege, and that to imply they had would be a lie. After further discussion, leaders agreed and then proceeded to tell the students the truth, expressing both pride in them for having come so close and certainty that success was just around the corner.

In the following week the two classes had more than 95 percent attendance and the students truly earned their privilege. As a team, administrators had a serious conversation about whether they had believed that the students could reach agreed-upon targets. They certainly believed it once the students had proved it!

Belief in students. When people recall their most memorable teacher, they often think of one who demonstrated unwavering belief in the individual's ability to achieve at a high level. But in most schools that feel powerless, the belief that most students can be successful is often missing.

An RTI Action Network report (Ahram, Stembridge, Fergus, & Noguera, 2001) noted that MRDC, an education research organization, conducted case studies in 2002 that showed teachers in struggling schools "can feel overwhelmed by what they consider to be the high needs of their students, and thus lower their own expectations for student performance" (para. 5). But numerous studies show that for students, this sense that teachers believe in them is a primary ingredient feeding their successes (Hoy, Tarter, & Woolfolk Hoy, 2006; Lumsden, 1997; Muller, 2001; Murphy, Weil, Hallinger, & Mitman, 1989).

Belief in self. Teachers who know they're effective have a belief that they can teach students and manage their behavior, and that the control over the learning process lies within the teachers (Tschannen-Moran, Woofolk Hoy, & Hoy, 1998). In other words, they have an internal locus of control.

Conversely, according to Tschannen-Moran and Woolfolk Hoy (2001), teachers who don't believe they are effective are unwilling to persevere when the going gets tough and are unlikely to bounce back when they experience a failure. These authors add that a low sense of self-efficacy affects "the effort teachers invest in teaching, the goals they set, and their level of aspiration" (p. 783).

The bottom line is that teachers with low efficacy work differently from teachers with high efficacy in terms of how they demonstrate academic press with students. They simply do not hold the same level of expectation that students who are difficult or at risk will be successful in their classroom.

Belief in colleagues. Additionally, in a distressed school, effective teachers often remain unconvinced that their peers or their leaders are able to be equally competent. Oh, Kim, and Leyva (2004) found that teachers in struggling schools felt unsure about the efficacy of their peers, which "points to low collegiality and collaboration" (p. 69). In a school that feels powerless, a collective sense of efficacy tends to be absent, a deficit that can lead to a self-destructive cycle.

Belief in the school. This response by the adults in a troubled school—lowering expectations not only of themselves, but also of those with whom they work (both students and adults)—has a negative impact on the culture of the school by reinforcing the belief that *collectively, we do not have the capacity to be successful.* A sense of hopelessness sets in. Following the example of the teachers, students become unlikely (or unable) to believe in one another or to hold each other accountable.

Such a school may officially subscribe to high standards, but the simplistic prescription of high standards as a magic pill to fix everything in a school that feels powerless may do more harm than good. The standards must be accompanied by a strong *belief* that these standards will be attained.

Part II offers further thoughts about building staff and student efficacy and a sense of having power, and about establishing the belief that higher standards can be realized. Higher standards and a belief that everyone can reach those standards are not enough in a school where people feel powerless unless clear support systems are in place to help *everyone* attain these standards.

Social Support

Social support refers to helping students get their academic learning within the school from each other and from adults in the school (Lee et al., 1999). Social support must apply to both academic achievement and emotional well-being to "support the development of a child who is healthy, knowledgeable, motivated, and engaged" (ASCD, 2004, p. 3).

To enhance social support, the community can be brought in to contribute to the safety net that helps at-risk students move toward the goal of graduation. Social support is important because, according to Edeburn (2010), students are more willing to learn when they have positive relationships with people at school who believe in them.

Similarly, students have better educational outcomes when they feel known, cared for, and supported in their development, both emotional and social (Lee et al., 1999; Osher et al., 2007). Students whose graduation status is tenuous *must* have a sense that they are cared for and supported. They must be provided with opportunities for meaningful participation and assistance, and be assisted in developing a vision for the future (Benard, 1991).

Factors that contribute to social support allow students from damaging environments and relationships to develop healthy plans, including graduating (Shepard, Salina, Girtz, Davenport, & Broekhart, 2010). Without a sense of hopefulness, why would students—or staff, for that that matter—be engaged in the learning process?

So often in a low-achieving school, teachers go through the motions of teaching and students go through the motions of learning, but there is no real connection to high expectations, a belief regarding meeting these expectations, or specific action steps to make achievement of expectations a reality. Social support is where the head and the heart come together.

In some beleaguered schools, test scores actually decrease during the school year. Such schools are often overwhelmed by district office data telling them specific areas in which improvement is required. Staff work diligently—going over the data, aligning curriculum, and identifying areas to work on—in an attempt to implement higher expectations to meet these goals. Yet test scores still go down.

This result of test scores declining during the year aligns with the findings of Lee and Smith (1999), who observed that "schools with high levels of academic press do leave some students behind—those students who have little support to draw on from their teachers, their parents, their peers, or their neighborhoods. . . . These students are in trouble academically" (p. 936). It appears that as formal leaders push harder for better results without offering intentional support in meeting those standards for students *and* teachers, the most vulnerable may be harmed.

Specific systems of support at all levels that uphold students and teachers in meeting targeted growth plans are lacking in schools where people feel powerless. The bottom line is that *students (and teachers) are more likely to achieve educational goals if they have positive relationships within the schools* (Durlack, Dymnicki, Taylor, Weissberg, & Schellinger, 2011; Noddings, 1997; Dixon & Tucker, 2008).

The behaviors of listening, providing feedback, and consistently helping students with their work are the building blocks of both academic press and social support. They send a message to students suggesting that as a school, *we believe in you* and *we will help you*. After one struggling school had implemented supportive strategies for a year, students reported the following:

- "They (teachers) used to tell us we could do it but now they are putting in the time to help us. Now they are really doing it."
- "They take the time to show us that we are doing better."
- "We used to think that we couldn't do it. Now we know we can."
- "We have more connections with teachers this year. They are like parents. I am not saying that they didn't care before, but now we are able to form bonds."
- "Last year we would take tests and not do well. [The teachers would provide] one example and move on; now we can really learn it."

It appears that, from students' perspective, an underlying theme was that *time* was a powerful factor used to demonstrate social support. That is, by giving time, teachers and administrators sent a message that they cared and were committed to the students' success.

Feeling cared for makes all the difference. As Lange and Sletten (2002) noted, at-risk youth need relationships with people at school who have faith that they can succeed. Dixon and Tucker (2008) asserted, "The powerful experience of mattering to others is an essential aspect of healthy emotional and social development" (p. 126).

Theodore Roosevelt famously said, "No one cares how much you know until they know how much you care." At schools that feel powerless, what is striking is the power of intentional social support, which often translates as care, at all levels—schoolwide, parent/community-to-student, student-to-student, and teacher-to-teacher—to assist students and teachers in meeting learning expectations. Let's discuss what goes on individually when social support is implemented.

Schoolwide Social Support

It is important for students to connect with the school in a broader way than simply through their course work or the desired learning outcomes. Students need to see themselves having a role in creating a culture of pervasive caring. Whether it be through clubs, school activities, or helping out in schoolwide endeavors, contributing to the culture of the school gives students a sense of belonging.

According to Bryk and Driscoll (1988), schools that are genuine communities pay attention to the experiences of students in all areas, not just in the academic realm. These authors' work demonstrates that school traditions, along with shared values and attitudes, act as connective tissue in a school. Building a sense of school as a community in which students are treated fairly, are known in a positive way by students and peers, are recognized as having something to offer, and are actively supported in their success is the goal of social support.

At one low-achieving school, the new turnaround principal walked into the homecoming assembly to find the gym packed with what appeared to be every student in the school. He commented to another administrator, "I didn't realize we had so many students." The assistant principal replied, "Isn't it great? These kids really get fired up for homecoming." The principal's response: "Wouldn't it be nice if this many students showed up for class and were this excited about learning and graduating?"

The principal later initiated discussions with the leadership teacher and with students about ways to achieve the same level of participation in classes that had been demonstrated for pep assemblies. The idea caught on. Soon class competitions centered on attendance, discipline referrals, and the number of students passing their classes.

Class advisors and students were more active in helping each other to remember to come to school, assisting with homework, and providing each other with strong doses of encouragement offered through both words and tutoring sessions. Specific programs that build social support in a school are discussed in a companion book, *Powerless to Powerful: School Systems Change*; but the point here is that if the adults put the spotlight on what is important, the students will follow.

Creating a caring environment is not about facilitating random activities found in typical homecoming events. Rather, a caring environment is grounded in embracing the big ideas of social support and then applying them to the context of your school. Building an amicably competitive environment and keeping score schoolwide works, but the key is to be sure that the competition and the scorekeeping are centered on what is important.

Schoolwide systems of support must be present to support the whole child in his or her academic achievement, behavior, and social-emotional needs. These support systems operate teacher-to-student, student-to-student, and teacher-to-teacher.

Teacher-to-Student Social Support

Teachers' beliefs about their students are an important element of social support, according to Bryk and Driscoll (1988) and Bryk, Lee, and Holland (1993). These researchers reported that teachers who showed warmth by talking with students about the students' personal and social lives were more likely to be caring in the classroom as well, resulting in students' feeling supported.

Once such connections are made, the school begins to feel like a family; an increased sense of belonging is created, which is an important element of high-achieving schools (McWhirter, McWhirter, McWhirter, & McWhirter, 1998, as cited in Fitch & Marshall, 2004).

Administrators who work in schools that feel powerless have found that an easy way to determine whether a student has a positive connection with a teacher is to ask the student three basic questions:

- Are you learning?
- Does your teacher like you?
- Do you get help when you need it?

Answers to these three powerful questions reveal how the student is feeling toward his or her learning not only in the classroom, but also schoolwide. Teachers find the answers fascinating, and they work to make the answers ones that show learning is taking place.

These same questions, slightly adapted, can be revelatory in terms of how staff perceive their relationships with administration and the school. They can ask themselves:

- Am I learning and growing as an educator?
- Does my administrator respect me?
- Do I get help when I need it?

Smith and Lambert reported in 2008 that Raymond Wlodkowski researched a tactic called "two-by-ten." In this strategy, teachers spent two minutes talking with the most difficult student in the classroom about anything the student wanted to discuss (as long as it was appropriate). Teachers did this for ten days in a row. Wlodkowski found that overall behavior in the classroom improved, and the behavior of the individual student improved 85 percent.

Smith and Lambert concluded that "when we internalize the assumption that students want to learn and participate, we begin to see that beneath their complaints about the lesson, homework, or seating chart, students are saying one thing: 'Please care for us today'" (p. 143).

Once the foundation of a caring relationship has been established, students will be far more eager to learn. Our job is to be aware of and facilitate that desire by providing the desired attention.

Employees within the school have to demonstrate emotional connection before they can expect students to apply themselves academically. Staff can use the strategy of giving positive, personal attention to troubled students within the first month of school. Counselors can list the names of all students who are not on track to graduate. Teachers can select students whom they know well, whom they believe they have a positive relationship with, and who are *not* in one of their current classes, and implement the two-by-ten strategy.

The result of focusing time and attention on select students is that not only do targeted students behave better and attend more consistently, but also positive relationships develop among staff as the strategy inspires increased cross-communication within and across grade levels and content areas. Furthermore, students see teachers trusting teachers. Students are motivated when they see teachers communicating more—and know that it is about *them*.

Increased and individualized attention must be coupled with high expectations. Caring teachers and administrators need to let students and parents know that they are expecting and helping students to succeed. As associate director of the New Teacher Center Gary Bloom noted, "They harass and harangue; they don't give up; they advocate relentlessly for students. It needs to be more work for a student to fail than it is to get onboard" (as quoted in Krovetz, 2007, p. 93).

Krovetz (2007) added that in a school where teachers and administrators have high expectations,

> Students who need academic support are accelerated (helped to catch up), rather than remediated (too often associated with falling further behind). Only when we have high expectations and purposeful supports for our students will all students have a sense of the future that is optimistic and hopeful. This requires that teachers and administrators believe, say, and practice for all students: "This work is important. You can do it. I won't give up on you. I am here to support you." (p. 93)

In other words, the students are not alone in their journey. The expectations they long to hold for themselves are first held, and communicated, by their teachers.

High expectations and support are not only for students. Although the research continually reminds us of the importance of teachers caring for and supporting students, it is equally important for formal leaders to care deeply and support their teachers in ways that include the development of schoolwide systems that assist teachers in actualizing their mission of helping each student be successful in her or his work.

Teachers must work supportively with students; equally, administrators must work supportively with teachers. And then, students are asked to work supportively with one another.

Student-to-Student Social Support

Students and teachers manifest the power of student-to-student social support. Once students understand that the adults in the school care and are really there for them, they begin to spread that caring to one another.

After the new support programs had been implemented at one low-achieving school, a student observed that the difference was notable, saying, "We started to care about other people too. You could hear people say, 'Come to class.' 'We *want* off-campus lunch.' 'Get your grades up. You can graduate!'" Another student reported that if a student was not on track to graduate, "everybody tries to support them to help them." Students also participated eagerly in a peer-mentoring program in which advanced mathematics students tutored those who were behind.

When staff *and* students intentionally develop student-to-student social support, a culture for learning is fostered. That culture is enhanced through the implementation of a comprehensive, results-oriented counseling program, discussed in greater detail in *Powerless to Powerful: School*

Systems Change. In this program, students are actively monitored and supported by the counseling department in achieving the necessary requirements for graduation.

Using data not to punish but to inform is the first step in developing student social support. Let students know, in an intentional way, that their help is needed in turning around a school that feels powerless. Teach students about the power of social support—let them in on the secret. Have frank discussions with all student groups in the school about what you as a school are trying to do; solicit their ideas about how they can help each other stay on track to graduate.

When formal leaders and teachers intentionally share data with students, they'll be amazed by what students will do to support each other. For the adults, the trick is to get out of the students' way once this train has left the station. When data is shared with students at low-achieving schools, youth start texting friends to remind them to get to class on time, giving each other rides, helping each other complete important requirements such as senior projects, and cheering for each other and their collective successes.

All students want to graduate as badly as the adults in the school want them to. Unfortunately, many students have learned behaviors that make it appear that they don't care. So many students in a school that feels powerless have learned a sense of hopelessness. Social support—specifically student-to-student social support—is one of the beginning points to rekindle a spark. Administrators in such schools often notice that when student-to-student social support increases, teachers actually offer more social support to their students.

In one case, perception surveys given at the end of the first year of implementation of support systems confirmed that teachers believed students cared more about their learning than they had in the past, and that students believed teachers cared and supported them more in their learning. Ideally, students can model their support of one another on the collegial behavior of teachers in the school (Lee et al., 1999).

Teacher-to-Teacher Social Support

Students don't want to be engaged if they sense their teachers aren't engaged. Research shows that student engagement is determined to a great extent by the "quality of the interactions among and between students" (Harper, 2009, p. 1) and by expectations shared between teachers (Lee & Smith, 1999). Often in a school where people feel powerless, teachers rarely communicate with or support each other in developing and implementing quality behavioral management systems or viable curriculum.

Students know when teachers don't get along professionally. Unprofessional relations sometimes result in teachers' actually undermining each other. Teachers must engage with, believe in, and support each other—privately and publicly—if the school is to develop a culture for caring.

An effective way for teachers to engage with one another is through the venue of professional learning communities (PLCs). As former teacher and principal Rebecca DuFour explained in a 2009 video posted by Solution Tree in 2013, the purpose of PLCs is to "build a collaborative culture. We take collective responsibility for the success of all of our students. And we use results to drive our efforts, to let us know whether what we're doing is truly making a difference."

PLCs give teachers a focused venue in which to brainstorm, take risks, and reconnect with one another and with their enthusiasm for teaching. The role a professional learning community plays in the transformation process is discussed more fully in *Powerless to Powerful: School Systems Change*.

In summary, the notion of social support is based on the idea that if students have more personal connections, more interactions in which they are recognized as individuals, they will achieve more. For this reason, Mussoline and Shouse (2001) suggested that schools be restructured in a way that allows them to act as supportive, collaborative, and interdependent teams.

Academic press and social support are both necessary to improve student performance. Yet, essential though they are, they are not enough. The element that binds them together and creates interdependence and synergy is relational trust.

Relational Trust

Trust between members of an organization grows when roles are clear and each person can depend upon the others to do what they are expected to do, and when each person is listened to and treated respectfully (Bryk & Schneider, 2003). The quality of the daily interactions between members of the school is the ground that determines whether relational trust flourishes (Bryk & Schneider, 2003).

Schools are organic entities in which alliances must be nurtured. The relationships between all stakeholders in a school have an impact on how they perform. Relational trust, built between participants through day-to-day interactions (Bryk & Schneider, 2003), is not simply a feeling of affection, but the conscious regulation of one person's dependence upon another (Zand, 1997) coupled with "reliance on another's good will" (Baier, 1986, p. 234).

According to Bryk and Schneider, *relational trust* is built in the "interrelated set of mutual dependencies" (p. 20) that exist in a school when people have role clarity and meet one another's expectations regarding the obligations of those roles. Bryk and Schneider noted that "trust among teachers, parents, and school leaders improves much of the routine work of schools and is a key resource for reform" (p. 114).

This sentiment was echoed by Goddard, Salloum, and Berebitsky (2009), who stated that schools at their core are social institutions whose success is dependent on the character of the relationships fostered within them. They added, "Many efforts to understand and improve academic outcomes for all children fail to focus directly on the important link between the quality of school social relations and the effectiveness of teaching and learning" (p. 293).

These researchers appear to suggest that relational trust is embedded in both academic press and social support working together; and that it grows when clarity of roles and responsibilities is coupled with high expectations that everyone will perform his or her role—that leaders will lead well, teachers will teach well, and students will achieve high standards.

These expectations are grounded in an environment that is safe for everyone and in which all stakeholders depend upon and have *faith* in each other, exemplified through *actions and words*. A sense of fidelity toward each other results in staff, students, and formal leaders working together toward the goals of the school: quality teaching and learning. In other words, a culture exists that promotes *everyone's* learning and growth.

The power of relational trust—whether between teachers and students, teachers and teachers, or administrators and teachers—is the foundation for transformational change. Patrick Lencioni's *The Five Dysfunctions of a Team* (2002) describes the building blocks necessary for developing a culture that results in high performance.

Lencioni's model points out that if trust between team members is absent, it will be impossible for a team to embrace conflict. If conflict is not viewed as an opportunity to solve problems, then differences become a reason for people to begin to blame each other for the failures of the organization.

In a school where conflict is high, teachers continually run for cover by isolating themselves or by forming coalitions. The blame begins with finger pointing at colleagues and administration. Without effective problem solving, colleagues are unlikely to achieve consensus and commit to common goals. Without commitment, they are unlikely to embrace a sense of personal and group accountability. And without accountability, the organization will continue to get the same results—or worse.

Many of the attributes that Lencioni (2002) described are present in a school that feels powerless. There is little trust between parties: Students are not considered capable, administrators do not believe in staff, and certain factions of the staff do not believe in each other.

In such a school, frustrations are high due to the failure rate, and the ability to solve problems is significantly diminished. People feel alone in their efforts to achieve the goals of the organization, which results in deep-seated fear regarding commitment to and accountability for new "agreements" that feel as if they come from the top down rather than being agreed upon by the group.

Staff and formal leaders are actually fearful of being punished if achievement does not improve. Consequently, not only does the school get poor results, but achievement results may actually go *down*. If Lencioni's (2002) five dysfunctions are not addressed within a school that feels powerless, the school not only will continue to lack power, but it will also become broken and be put out of business.

The ideal situation, of course, is that trust is high, people embrace conflict, and creative problem solving is used to seek out new commitments to excellence that are made with a sense of individual and group accountability so that continuous improvement and improved results are demonstrated (Figure 1.1).

If relational trust is to be jump-started in a school where people feel powerless, three factors need to emerge as a result of specific behaviors of the formal leaders, according to Bryk and Schneider (2003). Staff must:

1. Feel safe;
2. Perceive that the leaders have something to offer; and
3. Believe that the leaders will put in the time to help them be successful.

Figure 1.1.   Essential elements in a functional school. The absence of these components is what Lencioni (2002) called the five dysfunctions of a team.

Over time, relational trust will deepen between administration and teachers as well as between teachers, resulting in the relationships' being seen as mutually beneficial. Then people feel safe and will work together on common goals and outcomes.

ACADEMIC PRESS, SOCIAL SUPPORT, AND RELATIONAL TRUST WORKING TOGETHER

The research cited in the previous sections seems to imply that relational trust acts as both a catalyst for and an outcome of the union of academic press and social support. When relational trust grows because roles and responsibilities have been clarified in an environment in which people have high expectations and believe each other will perform, relational trust increases still more.

When that happens, people are more willing to be held accountable for the steps along the way as they move collaboratively toward mutually held organizational goals. Figure 1.2 illustrates the nature of the relationships among academic press, social support, and relational trust. This conceptual framework is accurate for all levels of interactions within the school, regardless of age or role of the participants.

Often the lines between academic press, social support, and relational trust become blurred. Academic press and social support are equally important; where the spotlight shines most brightly determines the nature of the conversation. If the emphasis is on curriculum work, that is, what we want students to know, or if it's on behavioral management, then the spotlight is on academic press. Asking *What will we do if our students do not perform well, either academically or behaviorally?* focuses work around social support.

Cultural shifts take place when questions related to academic press and social support are being asked simultaneously, and when our behaviors and beliefs are rooted in relational trust. Then we feel safe with each other, demonstrate a willingness to put in the time to help one another, and recognize that what we have is valuable and meaningful to each other.

At this point the circles of academic press and social support begin to overlap, resulting in a cultural shift that supports and challenges everyone to learn and be their best selves.

The interaction among each of the factors found in the conceptual framework is what leads to a real cultural shift in a school that feels powerless. But it is not simply the interaction that is important; it is also the balance among the framework's elements.

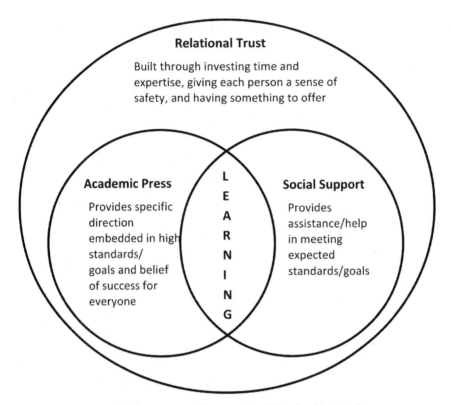

Figure 1.2. Our optimal conceptual framework. All levels of interactions among academic press, social support, and relational trust are displayed. (Salina, 2013)

Lee and Smith (1999) found that academic press without social support resulted in negative effects for some students. The same was true for students in schools that had a low level of academic press, regardless of the level of social support. As Lee et al. (1999) explained, if they are "to succeed in schools that press them hard to learn, students need strong social support. Conversely, even in the presence of strong social support, students will not learn much unless schools press them to achieve academically" (p. 3).

In schools where academic press and social support are strong, the behaviors of relational trust are also evident. People in these schools feel safe, believe in each other and what each has to offer, and put in the time to get the desired results. Ideally, the three components of academic press, social support, and relational trust will not merely overlap somewhat, but will be united entirely to maximize student learning.

The conceptual framework is easy to describe, but it's difficult to actualize if systems are not in place that facilitate academic press, social support, and relational trust. In other words, a culture that promotes the learning and growth of each member is intentionally developed through systems embedded in academic press, social support, and relational trust.

Systems within a school that possess all components of the conceptual framework are centered on *achievement orientation, behavioral management, and social-emotional needs*. A systems approach based on this conceptual framework is outlined in the next section.

CHANGE FROM THE OUTSIDE IN

In *The 7 Habits of Highly Effective People,* Covey (1989) discussed the notion of purposeful change occurring from the inside out, suggesting that effective people work on themselves and what they can control before orchestrating change in their environment and in those with whom they work. In a school that feels powerless, quick and dynamic change starts from the *outside in.*

In such a school, a great deal of pressure is placed on classroom teachers to improve student learning. Data is considered an enemy instead of a friend—it is perceived as a threat. Teachers in these schools are constantly being told to improve curriculum, instruction, and assessment practices to raise test scores. Important opportunities of time are spent in professional development with external consultants telling educators ways to improve.

Much of the change in schools today is program driven. Implicit in this process is that teachers are being told that what they have been doing is not good enough or that they don't know how to do their work. Very little time is given to staff for sense making.

Teachers go back after trainings, try to implement the new program with little support or feedback regarding ways to improve, and continue to get the same, or sometimes even worse, results. Much of this work is done in isolation and is doomed to failure. Instead of being in a process of continuous improvement, schools that feel powerless are in the *cycle of continuous failure,* with no strategies evident that would alter the course.

Many of today's programs and trainings focus on the practices of the classroom teacher in an effort to improve student learning. The classroom is without a doubt the environment that has the greatest potential to improve learning. Unfortunately, in a school that feels powerless, the classroom is not always the best place to begin the *school* improvement process.

If people in a hurting school are to regain their confidence and sense of control, school change must transpire from the *outside in.* Until intentional schoolwide systems have been implemented to support the work of departments and classrooms, a cycle of failure will continue. Why would staff stick their necks out once again to be told how to do the work, left to do it without support, and blamed for poor results? Little wonder that when external pressure is on and the results aren't good, fingers point outward.

Formal leaders working with staff in creating and implementing schoolwide systems send a message to the teachers: "I recognize the importance of your work, and I trust in your ability to do it."

Furthermore, when formal leaders implement schoolwide systems and ensure that those systems are doing what they are intended to do by monitoring and adjusting them based on current needs, relational trust results because the behavior is grounded in helping others in a way that's focused on their needs. Developing relational trust between staff and administration through the implementation of schoolwide systems is the first step in fostering academic press and social support at all levels in a low-achieving school.

Formal leaders must take responsibility for initiating change in a troubled school. Often administrators make comments reflecting this sentiment: "I have to get the right players on the bus before I can begin change." Yet the power also lies in the bus driver's knowing where she or he is taking the bus and how to drive it.

Getting everyone to the destination safely and in an orderly fashion is critical. When the bus driver conveys clearly where the bus is going and the riders are vested in the final destination, a journey begins in which individuals connect and figure out where they fit in and how to contribute. The riders on the bus play an important role, but positive change begins with leadership demonstrated by the bus driver.

Effective formal leaders of a struggling school identify and implement schoolwide behavioral, social/emotional, and achievement systems that support the work at both the department/grade level and the classroom level. At each level, the focus is on developing these same types of systems. Work schoolwide is centered on interventions focused on behavior, social-emotional support, and achievement. Schoolwide systems must be initiated before change will take place at the department, grade, or classroom levels.

Much of the work at the department/grade level takes place when PLCs focus on bolstering student achievement, identifying common standards, conducting collective assessments, improving instructional practices, and finding ways to support students to be successful. Classroom systems include many of the same elements, but they focus on the individual level, aligning the student's work with the department/grade level and with schoolwide systems.

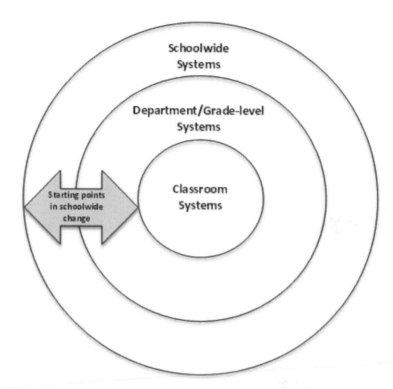

Figure 1.3. Development of relational trust. All educational systems must be involved to foster academic press and social support.

The important point is that all systems are aligned in answering the same questions:

- What do we want our students to learn?
- How will we know if our students have learned?
- What will we do if they have already / have not learned? (DuFour et al., 2004, pp. 2–3)

What's different is the nature of the work and who is responsible for what at each level in answering these questions. The systems at each level are anchored in the conceptual framework of academic press, social support, and relational trust. Consequently, when the systems are aligned within the conceptual framework, interdependence and a sense of mutual accountability will be present; unique sets of roles and responsibilities will be defined and understood by all.

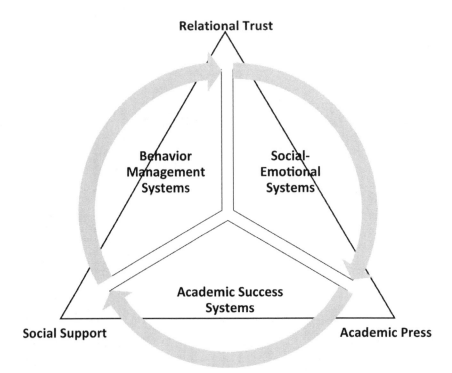

Figure 1.4. Alignment of systems with conceptual framework. Systems must be aligned with the framework to foster independence and mutual accountability.

As schoolwide systems and expectations are being developed, so too are department/grade level expectations as the process becomes dynamic and each level influences the others toward the desired outcomes. Alignment is always undergoing change and is driven by the needs present at the classroom level. When schoolwide and department/grade level alignment is achieved, then rapid change will occur in the classrooms because individual teachers will see the collective whole working together to support their efforts.

Embedded within each of the systems are clear and high expectations, support of each other in meeting these expectations, and trust that each will fulfill his or her expected roles.

Now it is critical to understand the lessons regarding the behaviors the leadership needs to learn to be able to implement such systems. Part II includes hard-earned insights about fostering relational trust, developing high expectations, and creating support systems to achieve these expectations.

Part II

Leadership Lessons Learned

Leadership in a school that feels powerless is about facilitating change that moves the school from its current reality closer to a collective ideal. If they are to do this work successfully, formal leaders cannot lead in the same way they did decades ago.

A lot of high schools in our country are experiencing difficulties; yet they are still operating the same way as they did more than thirty years ago—with counseling offices as career centers, six-period days, credits based on seat time; things look the same, right down to the desks in the classroom.

At the same time, the high expectations for learning new core content are being felt in our schools. Demand for change feels quick now because we as a profession have not evolved and made the necessary adjustments over time to meet the needs of today's learners. Consequently, schools are significantly behind in addressing the needs of staff and students alike.

Developing a culture for learning in redefining a school that feels powerless requires a special skill set on the part of the formal leaders. Formal leaders must be able to see the collective whole and the individual parts within it. So how does the formal leader inspire change, reconnect staff to their purpose, and animate a shared vision that meets the needs of today's learners?

These are questions stakeholders in a school might ask:

- Does the leadership team have a firm understanding of staff members' perceptions of our current reality and of what *their* ideals might look like?

- Does the leadership team believe that each staff person can be successful, and do they demonstrate behaviors that support that belief?
- Do leaders really listen to the staff in ways that inform the decision-making process and communicate a collective vision?
- Do staff understand how each person fits in and contributes to the well-being of the school?

A leadership team can start to foster change by examining their own behaviors and related beliefs to see whether they are sending a consistent message to staff. The next step for the leaders is to demonstrate new behaviors to change old beliefs held by the staff about leaders' commitment to helping each one of them achieve success.

This process can be reduced to a very simple formula:

BEHAVIOR + BELIEF = CONSISTENT MESSAGE

It is important to discern the behaviors and beliefs of leaders in a struggling school that need to shift if the school is to initiate a systems approach to change that is guided by the conceptual framework of academic press, social support, and relational trust.

When pressure is strong to get better student results, it's easy for leadership teams to forget the needs of staff. Their first instinct is to put more pressure and support on staff to do their work more effectively. Leaders must model for the staff the behaviors expected of them in working with the students. This part of the book describes the lessons learned about the behaviors and beliefs necessary to help staff rediscover their purpose and foster a schoolwide culture grounded in systems for learning.

LEADERSHIP LESSON #1: ONE-ON-ONE IS POWERFUL

Be intentional and focused in two-way conversations with staff to create an ongoing process that evokes understanding of the current reality, facilitates problem solving, and connects each person's talents to the vision of the school.

Kouzes and Posner (2012) point out that inspiring a shared vision is necessary if people are to move forward in a way that supports organizational goals and objectives. The more closely individuals' needs are aligned with the vision and the realities of the organization, the more likely those individuals are to be motivated and to construct meaning and purpose around their work.

Educational research demonstrates that if students are to be successful, every staff member must believe that each student is able to attain high expectations (academic press) and must offer systematic support in meeting these expectations (social support) (Lee et al., 1999; Lee & Smith, 1999). Parallel beliefs must be held by formal leaders regarding the staff.

Where does a formal leader start with this mission of helping the school rediscover its vision and reconnect each staff member to that vision and his or her own personal mission? Reconnecting people to their mission and the work of helping students learn begins by having teachers *define what they believe the work is* and *integrate their thinking* into how the school operates.

The key question that each staff member needs to respond to is: "What is it that gives your professional life purpose and meaning?" In this sense, change does start from the *inside out*—one staff person at a time (Covey, 1989).

In a low-achieving school, staff often feel misunderstood and unsupported by the formal leaders. They often make comments like these:

- "If only administration would listen and enforce the rules we have, we would be fine."
- "The district and the administration only worry about test scores. They don't understand the pressures of my classroom."
- "If only our students didn't have so many obstacles and barriers such as poverty, drugs, and single-parent households, teaching would be so much easier."

Administrators, too, can display a sense of learned helplessness, believing that *if only* teachers were more open to better ways of teaching and *if only* the district office could take into account the demographics of the school or the teachers' reluctance to change, then the district office and the community would understand the low test scores.

This blame game, especially in low-performing schools, has become a real cancer. If schools and student learning are to improve, then we need to remember what Jerry Garcia, the famous philosopher and rock star, once said: "Somebody has to do something, and it's just incredibly pathetic that it has to be us." So, where does the change begin?

The notion of the heroic leader who will ride into the school on a white horse to save the day is long gone. Nor can educational staff say, "I'm not the leader of the school. What can I do?" Again, Heifetz points out that leadership means influencing the community to face its problems and current reality together, and then developing a collective vision and plan to move toward that vision or ideal.

School transformation is everyone's responsibility. It is about building everyone's capacity to do the work. That's easy to say, but hard to do.

**Every organization has problems. The difference between effective orga-
nizations and those that fail is that the former have processes in place to
solve problems, and systems invented to assist the organization in successfully living its mission.**

The formal leader's role is to put the spotlight on the *right* problem, engage everyone in the process of problem solving, and collectively create
and implement structures and systems that address those problems.

The starting point in demonstrating new behaviors is for the leadership
team to *deeply listen, one-on-one, to each staff person on a regular and ongoing
basis*. These conversations promote new understandings, foster common
ground, and move the school toward problem solving and a call for action. One-on-one conversations develop relational trust, but more importantly, they build capacity and increase efficacy in those served.

One-on-one conversations should be conducted intentionally and
facilitated by the guiding questions of the leadership team. One-on-
ones can be a form of data collection rather than random conversations.
These talks can follow a specific line of inquiry and promote solution
finding. One-on-ones are not just for gathering information about how
the formal leader might help each staff person; they are about a specific
concern.

If the goal was simply to gather information every time a teacher said
"I need help," by the time the leader had met with each staff, she or he
would have an overwhelming number of "fires to put out" on behalf of
someone else that might not even relate to the overall well-being of the
school. Problem solving crises for someone else is not capacity building.

One-on-ones can foster capacity building through *helping* and *empower-
ing* others within a safe environment that promotes *problem solving* and
risk taking as well as a *willingness* for staff to be held *accountable* in their
areas of responsibility.

One-on-one conversations are grounded in the concept of being at least
dually beneficial: helping a staff person move toward his or her purpose
and at the same time helping the school move forward toward its vision.
One-on-ones focus on framing the school's current reality, envisioning
what the ideal may look like and figuring out the systems that need to
be in place to help make the shift between the status quo and the ideal.

Over time, these two-way conversations become more sophisticated
and take on their own form that builds on the vision of the school and on
the collective talents and individual needs of the staff. One-on-ones are
embedded in *all* of the Lessons Learned and will be discussed throughout
this section of the book. What follows are some basic strategies for jump-
starting the one-on-one process.

Basic Leadership Strategies

1. Divide the staff members up among the leadership team. Ask each team member to develop a lesson plan for success for each staff person assigned.

   Much like the way we ask teachers to diagnose their students' readiness to learn new information, we need to develop a lesson plan to assess each staff person's readiness to take on new work. As Glickman (1990) suggests, we must ask leaders to diagnose each person's level of commitment to the vision of the school and to outline the individual's competence levels or ability to solve problems.

   Remember, there can be *no favorites* in the one-on-one process. Formal leaders tend to go to the same staff over and over again for help or advice. Typically these staff members are seen as safe, and often they reinforce the thinking of the leader. Some staff see those people as the "favorites" or the "golden children," which only facilitates isolationism and the forming of coalitions.

   The key is making sure that one-on-ones are *inclusive*. Spend an equitable (not necessarily equal) amount of time with every staff member. In some cases, time may be spent listening to and understanding staff members who are the most bent and broken so that they can be reconnected to the school—even if those are the staff members who are the most trying.

   Often the staff member who may appear to be the most challenging has the most insight and is a powerful informal leader of the school. Listen intently to the message and the goal behind the message rather than focusing on how it may be communicated. The formal leader must be able to embrace conflict and differences without becoming defensive.

   As a formal leader, be open to new realities and listen to others' suggestions about how business might be done differently. Look for places of agreement and work from them. It is important for staff to *see their thinking at work* in system-wide change.

2. As a leadership team, develop a common list of questions to informally ask each staff person one-on-one. Have no agenda; just listen to how each staff person defines the current reality and what the ideal looks like from his or her perspective. The questions can be basic: What are we doing well as a school? What should we do differently? If you were captain of the world, what is one schoolwide change you would make to be more successful in your teaching? *Note: The focus is on schoolwide reform, not on instructional practice in the classroom.*

3. Reflect on what you hear and bring information back to the leadership team. Collectively look for themes and patterns in what teachers are saying. In initial one-on-ones, staff may express the opinion that the school lacks a behavior management plan and real support for students with social-emotional concerns and/or academic needs. Teachers may express hopelessness as well as feelings of being overwhelmed and alone in helping students.
4. Intentionally discuss with the staff, both one-on-one and in small groups, their perceptions of the current reality as identified by each of the themes. Be frank and candid—offer no sugarcoating and no blame. The ultimate goal in this process is to make sure the spotlight is shining on the right problem.
5. Begin to shape a call for action that defines what's next in moving toward a collective vision.

The profound impact of one-on-ones in a school that feels powerless cannot be overstated. One-on-one conversations become much deeper and more intentional over time. They are the foundational piece for continuous and ongoing improvement. They provide the leadership team with an opportunity to bounce ideas off of staff. *One-on-one conversations are not just about listening and learning—they are also about leading, educating, and influencing.*

After identifying common themes and problems brought up by the staff in one-on-ones, frame in a response grounded in the conceptual framework of high expectations and systems to support those expectations. Use lead-in statements such as: "This is what I am hearing from staff . . . Do I have it right?" and "Here are some ideas I have to address this . . . Do we have it right? What are your thoughts?"

This facilitation of two-way communication with the intention of finding common ground to work from assists in creating and implementing schoolwide systems that support the work of the departments, the grade levels, and the classrooms. One-on-ones help the leader diagnose the needs of the individual and the school. They also help to develop a common language that supports a line of inquiry that is intentional and focuses on moving from the current reality to a new ideal.

Demonstrate the power of this new behavior of having one-on-one conversations *daily with each staff member*: That is the starting point in making wise decisions and developing relational trust. Quite often, the longer someone has been involved in the work, the more likely that person is to prescribe rather than diagnose. Often leaders will, working in isolation, implement well-intentioned solutions with little input from those who will be affected.

Staff in a low-achieving school can feel like pawns in a chess match being moved around based on what the formal leaders think is the best way to address the latest crisis. Effective doctors ask a lot of questions of their patients to pinpoint the cause of the illness before prescribing a course of treatment. Effective leaders do the same. Take time to diagnose by asking the right questions and listening deeply to what colleagues are saying before starting to problem solve.

Coming to agreement about what the problem is can be far more difficult than developing the steps to fix it. Effective one-on-ones operate on the principle that it is wise to *go to the people who are closest to the work and will be affected by the decision.* The more formal leaders listen to staff, the more those conversations *shape the thinking of both the leaders and the staff* in developing a schoolwide vision and related action plans that include everyone's input and commitment.

The most valuable information comes from teachers when they are upset. Behind their complaints and concerns, staff identify the real issues and tell leaders what they need regarding schoolwide systems and support. This process is called *positive opposites*—taking a seemingly negative scenario and finding where meaningful, significant results could emerge.

Intentional one-on-ones are the bedrock for *all change* in a school that feels powerless. Use this strategy on a regular, ongoing basis. Effective leaders spend up to 50 percent of each day in such intentional conversations.

If one-on-ones are done correctly, a leader will never be surprised at a faculty or PLC meeting regarding what staff are thinking and what should be done; nor will staff ever be surprised by leaders' thinking, because there will be true common ground and a related plan of action created together.

It is through action teams or in a whole group that the fine-tuning of this thinking occurs. The one-on-one process is also the beginning point for leaders to demonstrate new behaviors to change old beliefs of staff. Leaders who take the time to listen to staff and integrate their thinking honor staff in the most important way. Over time, these conversations become more and more focused and intentional—especially after a 45-day leadership planning process is initiated.

These concepts and the planning process are further developed in the following lessons so the reader will have a clear understanding that the nature of the content of the planning process is constantly changing and that the ability to embrace change is fundamental to continuous improvement. The one-on-ones lead to a deeper understanding of the importance of intentional, ongoing planning and to clarification regarding who is accountable for what, which is Leadership Lesson #2.

LEADERSHIP LESSON #2:
INTENTIONAL ACTIONS INSPIRE HOPEFULNESS

A living plan of action that integrates what has been learned from the one-on-one and small-group processes must be created by the leadership team. The plan clearly identifies who is accountable and leads to intentional actions and systems that align with and support the work of the staff in helping students learn.

Most organizations, including school districts, have undergone some version of the strategic planning process. Typically in this process, (a) core beliefs are identified with vision and mission statements, then (b) related goals are written, and finally, (c) goals are elaborated upon with action plans, including timelines. These timelines tend to span at least a year, and leaders should plan to update them on an annual basis.

Quite often these plans are put on the top shelf, where they collect dust and have little to no effect on the people who do the actual work. If there is no plan, then the result is—as the tongue-in-cheek saying goes: *Having lost sight of our objective, we redoubled our efforts.* Many organizations that do not have a living plan in place become activity-bound rather than goal-driven.

Dwight D. Eisenhower stated, "Plans are nothing; planning is everything." The correct planning process adds clarity to the work and identifies who is responsible and accountable for that work. This concept of responsibility and accountability becomes an important topic of conversation among leadership team members—especially in the initial stages of the change process.

Assign responsibility to the person who does the work, and accountability to the person whose job it is to make sure the work gets done. It's like a baseball team. The manager is ultimately accountable for whether a team wins or loses, whereas the players are responsible for what happens on the field in their assigned positions.

The question to ask of the leadership team is: *What is each person willing to be held accountable for in improving student achievement?* This question may lead to a very dynamic conversation, and sometimes it's tough for team members to accept that indeed *they* are accountable for the goals found within the school improvement plan. Words of blame may creep into the conversation: *"If only . . .*"; *"should've . . .*"; *"could've . . .*"; *"I wish that . . .*".

But teachers will not declare what they, as a department or as individuals, are willing to be responsible and/or accountable for if leaders do not do the same. Once each person declares and owns what she or he is willing to be held accountable for within the planning process (academic press), it becomes clear that the individual can control her or his own destiny.

It's not about state or federal mandates, demographics, or teachers or parents who aren't doing their work; rather, the appropriate questions are: (a) What must I do in *my work* to ensure success in achieving a specific goal that I am accountable for? and (b) How can I help others on our leadership team as well as our teachers to do *their work* to support success in achieving that goal (social support)?

Leaders may wish to use a simple phrase to remind themselves of the importance of remaining connected to the vision of the school and that everyone has to take some level of responsibility: *Everyone has skin in the game.* The "game" is to achieve the shared vision of student achievement. This process also leads to role clarification and to an understanding that staff and administrators can rely on each other, and that it's okay to make mistakes along the way. This awareness begins building a deeper level of relational trust within the team.

The principal can reinforce the idea of having skin in the game by declaring to each person in the school, "If this school is not successful in moving forward in achieving our goals, then I should be held accountable for that failure. In other words, if you fail, I fail." The planning process clarifies each formal leader's area of accountability within the school. This clarification turns ideas and planning sessions into action in the school, and at this point change begins to take place at a very fast rate. *Doing nothing is no longer an option.*

Furthermore, it becomes critical for the principal to communicate to everyone that what they're doing doesn't have to be perfect, so that it becomes safe to try. The principal can put out the message that it's okay to falter and self-correct, but that it's not okay to do nothing!

When a school is feeling powerless, leaders do well to ask themselves: "What is the worst that could happen?" There is nowhere to go but up, a reality that gives rise to freedom among stakeholders to relentlessly and intentionally work together in aligning their actions in pursuit of the first "win." Schools grow as a team as staff and administrators come to realize that *they will either make themselves accountable or they will be made accountable by their circumstances.*

The planning process can be clarified by focusing the school improvement targets and related action steps on a small number of significant goals that are grounded in the feedback received in one-on-ones with staff. A simple leadership purpose statement that guides the planning process can be devised—for example:

> *As a leadership team we are intentional in our behaviors so that our work of initiating, monitoring, and evaluating schoolwide goals and actions will ensure higher student achievement and increased graduation rates.*

From the purpose statement, school personnel can create basic goals that, again, are grounded in information given by staff in one-on-ones. Here are some sample goals:

1. Strengthen a collaborative culture that both promotes student achievement and ensures that each student will graduate. Such a culture will be cultivated by individually and collectively focusing on the connection of curriculum, instruction, and assessment practices to improve student learning.
2. Relentlessly utilize data to refine and strengthen systems of social support and academic press for each student that results in higher assessment scores and graduation rates.
3. Develop and implement more opportunities for students to help them connect to school and community, build positive relationships, and envision their future.
4. Engage local and school community in building relationships that promote the success of each student.

Related action plans and timelines are to be created around each goal. Each timeline marks a 45-day calendar period; thus the document is known as the *45-day plan*. This is a living document. It clearly outlines what actions each person will take and be held accountable for in the 45-day period. Further ideas for using the 45-day plan are presented in *Powerless to Powerful: School Systems Change*.

This is not a school improvement plan; this is the *leadership plan* that becomes school leaders' version of a *lesson plan* describing what each person is going to do to bring the school closer to its goals. Embedded in each time period are formative assessments, or *quick wins*. Quick wins are immediate successes a school can anticipate if each person accomplishes what he or she sets out to do.

The idea behind quick wins is that staff can see the leadership team demonstrating new behaviors in doing their work to support staff in doing *their* work in a very short time. Strategies to support these efforts are described next.

Basic Leadership Strategies

1. As a leadership team, reduce your vision to its simplest terms. Come up with a short phrase that describes your goal and use it over and over again in front of staff and students alike. In one-on-ones, ask staff and students basic questions such as: "As a school, what are we doing to help people achieve our vision *and* what are we doing that takes us away from achieving this vision?"

2. Find themes in the information you gather. Following are some examples of themes that may emerge from one-on-ones:
   - We need to trust each other in doing our work at all levels of the school.
   - Use data not to punish, but to inform our practice to support teachers and students.
   - Help students to go forward in their education after high school.
   - Reconnect the parents and the community so they will be engaged and support our students and the school.

3. Formulate specific goals (not too many; less is more) that support your themes. As a team, discuss what the goals mean to each person. Answer questions like:
   - What is our current reality?
   - What does success look like?
   - What would our ideal look like if we were living this goal?
   - What barriers do we face that prevent us from achieving our ideal?
   - Where do I fit in as a leader in helping the school to achieve this goal?

4. Based on the discussion, craft action steps for each goal; but be mindful in creating this action to list only what you believe you can accomplish in 45 days. If you develop a full year or even a semester, there will be too many details and it will become overwhelming. Schools move fast, and everything we do is formative: As we *do*, we learn, and then we adjust and do again.

5. Define who will be accountable for the overarching goal and/or action steps. This is a critical discussion, and the answer must be within the span of control of the leader who states, "I will be accountable for this specific goal and/or action step." The person who is accountable defines what a quick win looks like for the staff *and* the students.

6. Make the leadership plan visible to everyone. It's a good idea for the leadership team to meet in a large room where the updated plan can be transferred to chart paper and visibly displayed. Not only does this tactic allow the staff to see the plan, but it also allows the chart to serve as a visual reminder about the work for the next 45 days.

7. Embrace transparency. Complete transparency requires letting staff know when the 45-day plans are being developed/renewed and including *anyone* who wants to be part of the discussion. *No favorites!*
8. Remember, 45-day planning meetings are leadership meetings, *not* management. Time should be spent envisioning your future in concrete terms.

The 45-day planning process is a call for action. It's not about what teachers should do differently, but rather about what formal leaders are willing to do differently to ensure the success of staff and students. The following quote helps to illustrate the dynamic:

> Teachers are in the forefront of successful instruction; supervision [leadership] is the background, providing support, knowledge, and skills that enable teachers to succeed. When improved instruction and school success do not materialize, supervision [leadership] should shoulder the responsibility for not permitting teachers to succeed. (Glickman, Gordon, & Ross-Gordon, 1998, p. 7)

The leadership team will start to understand that the common vision of the school is theirs to own. Teachers are asked to differentiate to help each student succeed, so likewise, leadership team members must personalize what they want staff to know and be able to do to be successful. Teachers provide what students need; formal leaders provide what staff need (Hersey, Blanchard, & Johnson, 2012).

Leaders can ask themselves: *How will I as a leader be more intentional in how I use my time in helping each staff person I am responsible for to be successful in his or her work and in his or her area of responsibility and accountability?* School leaders must figure out how to slow down the work so that they make wise and intentional decisions to support the goals and action steps found in the 45-day plan.

Another baseball analogy is appropriate here. Spectators may wonder, "How is the player able to manage a ninety-six-mile-per-hour fastball or see a curveball coming toward him and still get a base hit?" Great hitters say that the ball seems almost to move in slow motion and that they can actually see the seams on the baseball. They have the ability to *slow the pitch down.*

It's the same for leaders. How can they slow the game so that they know what's coming at them in the school? As a leader, it is important to *know what you're looking for* and to monitor and adjust based on what's coming at you, as long as the adjusted behavior moves you toward the targeted goal. A great hitter gets a hit only about one out of every three times at bat. For a leader who feels she or he is "0 for 3," a specific school plan will lead the way in making wiser decisions.

When first the leadership team meets to start implementing the 45-day plan, they can discuss each person's plan for how time will be spent and what evidence will be collected to determine whether each has achieved the identified quick wins. Colleagues can share valuable information about what they have heard from staff regarding the goals, and discuss ways in which they can support the desired outcomes and communicate the big ideas, as well as gather feedback in their one-on-ones.

The second meeting is a good time to share successes. Successes are determined by the evidence collected, which is later used to establish accomplishments and future goals. Team members can share with the person who was accountable for the goal what they heard teachers saying, analyze key data points that informed *their* successes, and gather information on the next steps for the following week.

The person *accountable* for the goal is expected to lead the team in the discussion and to be prepared with relevant data and a proposed plan of action *before the meeting begins*. Lesson #4 will offer more information about how to develop a *problem of practice*. A cycle of improvement continues at the next week's meeting. These meetings can constitute a leadership team's PLC.

A leadership team's work must be grounded in an understanding that the success of the teachers is contingent on the leaders' behaviors that help the teachers provide quality teaching and learning opportunities for students. This understanding is evident in how leaders listen to the staff. Leaders become aware of how powerful the one-on-ones are in the planning process; questions and feedback become deeper with each staff person and lead in developing the 45-day plan.

Soon, staff members realize that the leadership team understands and cares about them and their success. The leadership team becomes more confident about being held accountable as they recognize that they have both support from peers and clear direction or a lesson plan for each week's work.

At this point, intentionality grows as the spotlight is put on the *right problems*. A new sense of hopefulness begins to emerge in the staff and the leadership team. Still, a 45-day plan is not enough. Time must be used to support the plan in a more intentional way—which leads us to Lesson #3.

LEADERSHIP LESSON #3: TIME IS GOLDEN

As a leader, use time wisely to identify, implement, support, and evaluate schoolwide systems that are aligned with the 45-day plan. This is essential in gaining relational trust from staff and is the beginning point in healing a school that feels powerless.

It's expected that as you implement your 45-day plan, you'll know where you want to go—but not how to get there. Remember, it is about learning *new leadership behaviors* to *change old beliefs of staff*. Formal leaders do well to embrace ambiguity and uncertainty. Fullan (2011) calls this "behave[ing] your way in" (p. 14). The journey heading true north is full of swamps and potholes that leaders have to navigate and avoid to arrive at the desired destination. *Heading true north in a straight line is impossible.*

Formal leaders and policy makers continually talk about the importance of instructional time, sometimes in regard to interruptions during instructional time or increases in the length of the school day. But not enough conversation has centered on how effective leaders spend their time facilitating change to develop a positive school culture. We might positively shift our learning cultures if we investigate how leaders spend their time during the school day.

One of the factors that results in leaders' gaining trust from staff in a dysfunctional school is the creation of schoolwide systems that support teachers in helping students learn. The important concept in Lesson #3 is that initially, the time used in a low-achieving school is focused more on *diagnosing and implementing systems schoolwide* that support teaching and learning at the grade or department level and in the classroom.

The development of systems sends a message to the staff that leaders believe in what they are doing and want to support them in doing it. Staff members already know what's not working in the school. When low-performing systems persist, teacher efficacy is low. Staff need to have someone who believes in them and challenges them so that a message is sent that they're capable of getting the work done. This message is sent when staff see their leaders spending time differently—in diagnosing, understanding, and implementing systems that support their work as identified in the 45-day plan.

The way to start this work is to have leaders analyze each role they play and the time they spend in each of these roles. The model pictured in Figure 2.1 may prove helpful in this process.

All four quadrants of the model are important in terms of how formal leaders spend their time. In analyzing their days, leaders may find that they spend much of their time in crisis management—putting out fires and trying to catch up to what policy and procedure say is important. Covey (1989) would say that these leaders are working in *urgent and important* mode. This mode is typically driven by panic, pressing deadlines, and a felt need to respond to outside forces.

Many leaders would claim that they dislike using their time in crisis management, but in reality that's probably what they know how to do best. Dealing with crisis is safe, whereas moving from the known (current reality) to the unknown (collective ideal), learning new behaviors, and leading are not. In a strange way, crisis becomes many formal leaders' comfort zone.

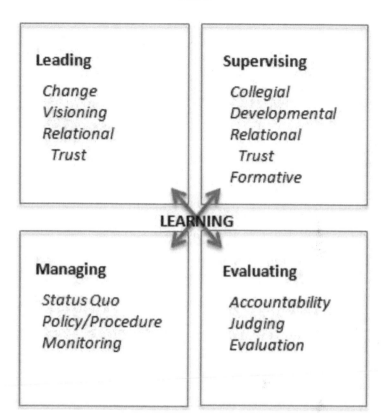

Figure 2.1. The four functions of administration. This is a model for how leaders spend their time.

In a perfect world, leaders would spend 30 percent of their time in the management realm and 70 percent in the realm of relationships, planning, and figuring out how to do business differently; yet the reality is often the exact opposite. Management is important, but much of it needs to be organized and preplanned in such a way that there is room and time for the real work of leading. Management and leadership should both take place in the *not urgent but important* quadrant.

If a leader simply manages a school, the school may maintain the status quo, but in today's world, maintaining the status quo means falling behind. To meet the demands of today's school, transformational leaders combine leadership and management in a way that produces healthy change. Many leaders get by for a while by being good managers, but that work doesn't meet today's demand for transforming schools. This may be one reason that administrators are frequently shuffled between buildings, often every three to five years: They've been effective managers but haven't created schoolwide change.

One assistant principal, asked why he spent so much time with groups of students in his office working on projects or helping them with their work, explained that he found it difficult to work with teachers and that it was easier to work with groups of students. He said that promoting school pride or helping students with problems was more doable than helping staff help students. But given that the nature of leaders' work is to support staff in facilitating change, he couldn't be effective if he was in his office working with students rather than in the school helping staff.

After a long discussion, leaders will probably agree that they would like to spend most of their time in effective leading and supervising.

Supervising is defined as capacity building—helping others to become self-supervised through building their sense of belonging to the school and their abilities in teaching and leading.

Covey (1989) would refer to activities that fall within this category as *important but not urgent*. Activities and behaviors in this category include visioning, relationship building, planning, having reflective conversations, and preparing to support the mission of the school.

In a school where people feel powerless, some of the leadership team members will admit frankly that at times they hide in their offices, feeling unsure of what their work is. Answering e-mails, writing reports, going to meetings, working with students—these activities are all familiar and feel safe. But it's not helpful for a leadership team to be busy if they're not helping staff.

Dwight D. Eisenhower gave a speech in 1954 in which he quoted the president of Northwestern University, J. Roscoe Miller, who said: "I have two kinds of problems: the urgent and the important. The urgent are not important, and the important are never urgent." In 1996, Covey, Merrill, and Merrill built a time management grid based on this idea.

Through studying Covey et al.'s grid, leaders may come to realize that creative tension exists among leadership, management, supervision, and evaluation. The idea is to use this tension and time to move toward a culture for learning so that leaders don't spend the majority of their time in the *urgent and important* quadrant.

Once this understanding is gained, leaders are likely to become committed to using their time to help staff by putting systems in place that support learning and promote a growth mindset. Leadership then is viewed not only as the process of developing a collective vision to enable

I m p o r t a n t	Urgent	Not Urgent
	I • Pressing Matters • Crises/Panics • Fire/Fighting • Deadline-Driven Projects	II • Prevention • Relationship Building • Planning/Preparation • Implementation of Systems • Professional Knowledge
N o t I m p o r t a n t	III • Interruptions • Some Call/Mail • Some Report/Meetings • Unprepared Meetings • Popular Activities	IV • Trivia • Busy Work • Time Wasters • Unproductive Activities (TV) • Everything Else

Figure 2.2. Time management grid (adapted from Covey, Merrill, & Merrill, 1996). In what quadrant do you spend your time in school?

others to act (Kouzes & Posner, 2012), but also as eradicating the "buffers" (Schmoker, 2006) that stand in the way of the schoolwide vision.

Note that a person can be stuck in *urgent and important* mode while leading, managing, supervising, and evaluating.

The trick is to move to *not urgent and important* when doing the tasks outlined in each of these quadrants. Administrators can discuss what *not urgent and important* looks like for each of them.

Basic Leadership Strategies

1. As a leadership team, develop working definitions for leadership, supervision, management, and evaluation. What behaviors would you demonstrate in your school for each of these categories if you were working in *urgent and important, not important and urgent,* and

important and not urgent modes? For example, *important but not urgent* behaviors may include the following:

   a. *Leadership*—sharing and planning with staff about *what is next* to improve the next 45-day plan well in advance.
   b. *Management*—developing next year's schedule, budget, and staffing that align with systems and building goals six months ahead of time.
   c. *Supervision*—having daily one-on-one discussions with individual staff to promote capacity building and connect their strengths to the 45-day plan and the goals of the school.
   d. *Evaluation*—developing a cycle of review at the beginning of the school year and having regular formative and summative assessments regarding how leaders hold themselves accountable as an administrative team.

2. Create a Four Functions of Administration grid. For the next three days, keep a running record of types of behavior you engaged in, according to your team's working definitions. Were you leading, supervising, managing, or evaluating? Which of the behaviors you recorded in each of the Administrative grids were *urgent but not important; urgent and important;* or *not urgent and not important* within a given category?

3. Ask yourself: *Was there a balance in terms of how I spent my time leading, supervising, managing, and evaluating?*

4. Review your 45-day plan. Identify behaviors you demonstrate in leading, supervising, managing, and evaluating that are in the *not urgent but important* category that will help you successfully implement your plan. Be clear and specific regarding the types of behaviors that will support your plan. Know that as you move from crisis to purposeful behaviors that support your plan, some behaviors will be *urgent and important.*

5. Practice these behaviors for a week. Come back as a team and discuss the following:

   a. What behaviors did I practice that allowed me to stay in the *not urgent but important* mode? What did it look and feel like when I was in *urgent and not important* mode?
   b. Did the *not urgent but important* behaviors require me to spend my time differently before and after school?
   c. Did I spend more time on leading and supervision than on management and evaluation?
   d. What effect did trying these behaviors have in terms of calendaring my time and how I communicated with the building secretary?
   e. Did the 45-day plan add clarity regarding how I spend my time?

f. As a team, what behaviors and uses of time brought us closer to implementing our 45-day plan, and what behaviors took us away from the real work as defined by our plan?

g. When do I believe it is important to work in *urgent and important* mode within each of the administration functions?

The intent of using the 45-day plan is to have leaders identify what is important for them to say and do to move the school closer to actualizing its mission. Self-examination regarding how leaders spend time to actualize these action steps is important if a team is to move the 45-day plan from paper to action. In Covey et al.'s words, it's wise to begin with the end in mind (45-day plan) and to prioritize actions (Time Management Grid in Figure 2.2). The process includes much of what teachers do in backward lesson plan design, where learning targets are clearly defined and curriculum/pacing is established to support learning.

A leadership team may decide that their goal is to spend, say, 70 percent of their time in proactive leadership and supervisory behaviors. In that case, leaders will have to be out of their offices and engaged in one-on-one conversation as well as in small groups that connect the staff and the work to the 45-day plan.

The school is likely to improve at a rapid rate as the administrative team becomes more effective at leading with purpose. Without management systems in place, leaders *cannot* lead and supervise. In fact, a lack of management systems results in leaders' working in *urgent and important* mode in all of the other three administrative factors of leading, supervising, and evaluating.

If a school is going to become great, leaders need to demonstrate new leadership and supervisory behaviors, both one-on-one and in small groups with staff. They need to have processes in place that engage staff in implementing the 45-day plan. This leads us to Lesson #4: Positive Opposites.

LEADERSHIP LESSON #4:
POSITIVE OPPOSITES—ACTION TEAMS

Engage teachers in developing, implementing, and improving schoolwide and classroom/departmental-level systems through action teams. Action teams are small groups of staff and/or students that identify their current reality and design a course of action to attain a new defined ideal.

As was mentioned in Lesson #1, when staff complain and point fingers, they are trying to define their ideal. Action teams can be used to develop a sense of optimism that also builds capacity and levels of trust between staff and among administrators. As formal leaders listen to staff, they should not be trying to convince the staff members to dig harder or telling them whether they're right or wrong. Listening deeply to the problem and knowing that it is not necessary to fix the problem, but rather to put the spotlight on the right problem—*that* is the work of a leader.

In his 1990 work, Glickman explained that effective teachers have a strong mission (commitment) and the ability to engage effectively in the problem-solving process (competence). In a school that feels powerless, teacher commitment, though perhaps waning, is still present, but often teachers seem less hopeful because problems appear too big to be fixed by individuals.

Formal leaders build capacity and lead partly by putting in place clear structures and processes that support staff to work in teams in such a way that they are able to proactively solve problems in a school. Effective leaders see problems as an opportunity to move toward the mission of the school; that's *positive opposites.*

As was mentioned earlier, it's important to be alert to the presence of common ground when listening to staff members. What are the themes discovered through one-on-ones and small-group discussion that are of concern to the staff? Not only are these themes the cornerstone of developing a 45-day plan, but they also become a focus in implementing *action teams.*

Action teams are short-term teams whose primary task is to find solutions to specific problems or barriers that are in the way of grade-level, departmental, or schoolwide goals. Action teams are the staff's equivalent of the leadership team's problem of practice process discussed in Leadership Lesson #2. One of the keys to building capacity is to help others become self-supervised by becoming effective problem solvers. Action teams are problem solvers.

Collaborative inquiry undertaken through action teams can provide a decision-making and problem-solving environment necessary to support long-term educational change (Giles & Hargreaves, 2006). Transformative learning won't take place within teachers unless they are "willing and able to critically explore, articulate, negotiate, and revise their beliefs about themselves, their students, their colleagues, and their schools" (Servage, 2008, p. 70).

Inquiry requires a particular stance toward experiences and ideas—"a willingness to wonder, to ask questions, and to seek to understand by collaborating with others in an attempt to" find answers (Wells, 1999, p. 121).

These underlying principles of inquiry and action teams are very similar to the underlying principles of a professional learning community. *However, an action team's primary focus is on schoolwide systems development and/or departmental/grade-level issues that are grounded in helping classroom teachers ensure that each student is successful.* Action teams are guided by the question: *What can we do differently as a school or a department/grade level in helping each other be successful?*

Action teams are not necessarily about improving instruction, curriculum, or assessment practices. This work is left to professional learning communities (whose role in change is discussed in greater depth in *Powerless to Powerful: School Systems Change*). Action teams are a great start in modeling for teachers how to behave in PLCs.

As described in Part I, teacher efficacy is low in schools that feel powerless. Teachers with low efficacy are less likely to believe that their work can make a real difference in helping each of their students learn. Initially, when leaders discuss ways to improve student learning within the classroom, teachers with low efficacy are overwhelmed and often become defensive. Finger pointing relating to attendance, behavior problems, or lack of administrative and parent support begins—and why wouldn't these teachers respond this way?

Teachers in low-performing schools are consistently reminded by district officials, politicians, and press releases that they are failing. Low-performing schools typically have many activities, but few well-thought-out systems to support the work of the classroom teacher. Teachers who are threatened and punished through poor use of data and the demand for quick fixes often push back and ask "What are *you* going do about it?" rather than asking "What can *I* do about it?" Action teams promote the question and response regarding what *we* are going to do as a school.

Action teams are an important statement from administration in moving from *me* to *we*.

When teachers have the foundation of action teams that assist them in supporting each student in being successful in their classrooms, they are more likely to begin digging deeper and harder. A sense of optimism, collaboration, and interdependence begins to develop, because isolation breaks down when staff members begin to feel ownership in student learning.

Consequently, the action team or problem of practice process is a line of inquiry that aligns schoolwide goals with departmental or grade-level needs and goals. The 45-day plan moves this alignment forward with a leadership plan of action.

The key to Heifetz's notion of leadership—influencing the community to face its problems—is that the leader must have the ability to make sure that she or he has identified the correct problem. This idea also implies that anyone who defines the problem and those who agree with that definition become the leaders. Most low-performing schools begin to break down when problem-solving sessions turn into gripe sessions in which everyone has different ideas regarding what the problem is and what should be done about it.

Lack of clarity and agreement about what the problem is leads to a sense of hopelessness, erodes trust between staff and formal leaders, and promotes the formation of coalitions. The staff member who talks the loudest, is effective in selling the problem one-on-one to colleagues, or refuses to join in is often successful in shutting down the problem-solving process.

Gaining basic buy-in about what the problem is from the majority of the people who are affected by the problem is the hardest step in the inquiry process. Heated conversations can develop among staff members about what the best *solution* is even when no consensus has been reached regarding what the *problem* is.

How many faculty meetings have you sat through about whether students should be allowed to wear hats or chew gum? In these discussions, how does a leader help staff to focus on the real problem, which may be *How do we as a school show respect and develop school pride?* The art of inquiry is to focus the real work on the current reality by asking:

- What do we want to move the school toward (ideal)?
- What are the barriers preventing us from moving forward toward this ideal?
- What processes might be put in place to get the desired outcomes (systems and goal alignment)?

Action teams must be both clear on the problem and goal-driven in order to define specific activities. Elements that are invented within an action team must support, influence, or build on the 45-day plan. *Most likely the work of action teams will be focused on systems creation and implementation that center on behavior management, student achievement, and/or social-emotional support.*

The important thing to remember concerning action teams is that what they create cannot be seen as an add-on or one more initiative that teachers "have to do" in their classrooms. Plans of action must be viewed as value-added in helping move to *the teachers'* desired outcomes.

Basic Leadership Strategies

1. The key to an effective action team outcome is framing in the right problem. Planning has to precede movement. Slower is faster. As Hersey et al. (2012) state, it is *ready, aim, fire* and not *ready, fire, aim.* Take the time as a leadership team to listen deeply to what the staff

say the barriers are, schoolwide or at their grade/department levels, that prevent them from being successful in their work.

Embrace what staff are saying without being defensive or providing facts in a way that suggests you're trying to convince them their thinking is right or wrong. Use the language of the 45-day plan in discussions with staff about the nature of the problem and existing barriers.

2. As a leadership team, openly discuss with each other and staff the information learned from one-on-ones. Leaders do well to ask individuals whether they believe leaders are getting the problem right. Typically, issues will be creating *schoolwide systems to support behavior management, increasing student achievement,* or *meeting the social-emotional needs of students.* Align the problem with a theme that is grounded in the 45-day plan. Once the nature of the problem and the related goals are understood, the rest will follow.

3. As a leadership team, evaluate existing programs and processes that may address the problem of practice or line of inquiry. How does this line of inquiry support or take leaders away from the 45-day plan? *If what is necessary is a simple and obvious tweak that you can make with existing systems, then as a formal leader, act!* If it is bigger than a simple fix and staff buy-in is crucial, then gather an action team to dig deeper into the problem of practice. The team should represent a cross section of the staff. Again, *no favorites.*

4. Be overprepared for the action team. Frame in the problem of practice in a way that influences the team regarding the problem and questions or structures that need to be in place for the school to move forward. Leaders who have done their homework in their one-on-ones are well-rehearsed in stating what the problem is and what the ideal may look like. In reality, what the leader is stating is coming from staff—they should hear *their thinking* in the *leader's words.*

There should be no surprises in an action team meeting given that relevant data has been gathered from staff and analyzed to jump-start the process. A good leader has also done one-on-ones with each person on the action team

At this point, the leader is sharing his or her best thinking arising from listening to staff. Holding an action team meeting as an open-ended forum that leads to meaningless brainstorming is unproductive. All that leads to is "Here we go again—lots of talk and no action." The action team cannot see this process as a waste of time; rather, the outcome must be perceived as leading to change.

5. Take the action team through the following protocol:
   a. Collectively identify the problem—the current reality.
   b. Provide relevant data about the problem. What data is available to clarify the problem? What other information is available?

   c. Reach consensus on what the ideal looks like, and be thorough
      as a team in describing what the action plan can be expected to
      accomplish. How will reaching the ideal help improve student
      learning in the classroom?
   d. Discuss solutions. What are the implications of research or rel-
      evant information? Which current practices may support the
      school's achieving the desired outcome?
   e. What barriers stand between the school and its ideal?
   f. Formalize a plan of action, being sure to include how score will
      be kept by tracking and analyzing identified results. Align the
      outcomes of the action team with the 45-day plan. Adjust the
      45-day plan if necessary. *How does the plan help improve one of the
      following: behavior management, achievement, or the social-emotional
      status of students?*
   g. Have action team members go out and, within PLCs and one-on-
      ones, discuss the outcomes of the action team. Gather more input
      if necessary.
   h. Do many one-on-ones, or *audits*, with staff to find out whether the
      action team got it right.
   i. If necessary, come back as a team and make changes based on
      feedback in moving forward.

Leadership and action teams can formalize the process in meetings
through 45-day plans and the related problems of practice by using the
worksheet (Figure 2.3) provided by the Office of the Superintendent
of Public Instruction (OSPI) from Washington State to jump-start their
thinking. Teams can also create a simple worksheet to describe their protocol or POP (problem of practice).

Action teams are intended to be *short-lived* (less than two weeks) and to
result in new behaviors on the part of both the leadership team and the
staff. Action teams address a schoolwide or departmental/grade-level
issue. Formal leaders' roles in this process are critical. Leaders cannot be
seen as manipulating or controlling the outcome; however, leaders must
be *tight on structures and processes* that lead to solutions and *action*.

Again, formal leaders must also continually audit and "tend the gar-
den" to see whether the plan of action is being implemented successfully. Small-group discussions and one-on-ones with all staff will reveal
whether the plan is working.

Successful leaders provide a strong dose of specific *positive feedback to
the people who are doing work* and *reflective conversations with people who are
not.* They connect the dots regarding meaning for those who are not buy-
ing in regarding how their skill set and strengths influence the well-being
of the school. Leaders must ask the difficult questions about why the

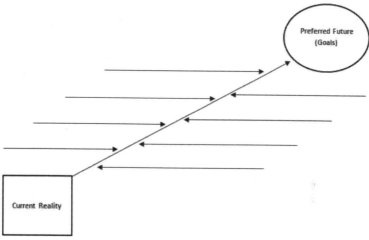

Figure 2.3. How to get to the preferred future. Worksheet from Washington State OSPI used by leadership and action teams.

expected behaviors are not being demonstrated and look for ways to help disillusioned staff live up to the expressed expectations.

Leaders do well to seek understanding. They should also refrain from jumping to conclusions about why any given staff member does not appear to support the plan. For a formal leader, it is important not only to encourage, but also to remind each staff member of the action agreement. Also, *leaders must be open to new realities. These staff members may have new information that could help improve the action plan.*

Leaders, your presence each day in every classroom and in high-traffic areas reminds the staff of what you believe is important. One-on-one audits can provide valuable information about what's working and what's not, and about how to modify and adjust the plan of action. Before shifting the plan of action, it's a good idea to make sure that changes are based not just on a few staff members' thinking about what's best, but rather on the wisdom that is provided by the collective whole.

Action teams are important vehicles for moving the school to new possibilities. In leading the process, be sure to be overprepared and to overcommunicate. Once the process has been modeled successfully and implemented by formal leaders, staff can be encouraged to come to the leadership team to propose possible action teams. The goal of developing action teams in solving a problem of practice is to lead to better ways of supporting the classroom teachers in doing their work. How do you know if your action plan is working? This leads us to Leadership Lesson

#5, which says that if something is worth doing, then it's smart to stay informed about its impacts by keeping score on what's important.

LEADERSHIP LESSON #5:
EVIDENCE IS EVERYTHING BUT NOT ANYTHING

As a school, become relentless in using the right *and* simple *sources of evidence that drive intentional, continuous improvement of schoolwide systems.*

A study done by William Parrett and Kathleen Budge in 2009 explored the actions leaders took to turn around high-poverty schools. One of the first things Parrett and Budge noticed was the implementation of accurate and useful data systems: "In fact, using data-based decision making was one of the two most common explanations offered for the schools' success" (p. 24). Improving a school through data-based decision making is possible only if accurate, appropriate data is collected intentionally and used effectively.

The other factor Parrett and Budge found to be present in high-poverty schools that improved student achievement was caring relationships. Academic press is key—and so is social support. Turnaround schools cannot expect to increase success if they have one without the other. Data can be a punishment or a prescription, depending on how it's used.

The schools with the best results "use data to identify students who need before, during, and after-school small group and individual tutoring; self-paced interventions using technology; one-on-one academic advising and coaching; homework support; or additional assessment time" (p. 26). In other words, data should be used to create systems that support the work of the teacher. Data can reveal trends and problem areas on a larger scale, giving much-needed insight about how educators can change, both in the classroom and schoolwide, to meet students' needs and improve achievement.

Using data to facilitate academic and social systems to support teachers and students is essential for a school that feels powerless. Consequently, it is important to understand what types of data are to be collected and how that data can best be used in planning. Data also gives direction regarding how leaders should be engaged in their work.

Schools aren't lacking data. One might argue that schools have too much data and are overwhelmed by trying to figure out what to do with all this information. DuFour, DuFour, and Eaker (2009) call this phenomenon "DRIP—data-rich, information-poor" (p. 99). As in action research, the nature of the question drives the types of evidence a researcher will collect.

The term *evidence* is perhaps more helpful than the term *data*. The term *evidence* can be more inclusive. When the word *data* is used, people often lock into the notion of achievement data, such as test scores, because of the current accountability trend resulting from educational policies such as No Child Left Behind and Race to the Top. Test scores are only one factor to use in analyzing where you want to go and how you want to get there on your way to building a culture for learning.

Perceptual data, evidence collected and organized into themes through the one-on-one process, may inform decision making at a much more powerful level than achievement data in helping a school that feels powerless to self-correct and invent systems to support learning. Four basic types of evidence collection are critical in the school turnaround process (OSPI, 2005). The key is knowing precisely which information will be helpful and what evidence will provide guidance in moving toward a defined ideal. The four types of evidence to collect are achievement, contextual, demographic, and perceptual.

Achievement Evidence

Achievement evidence on a school is readily available. Most states and school districts keep a running record on school success based on how well students perform on required tests.

In low-performing schools, teachers often dread the big reveal of last year's test scores. When the question *How did we do?* is answered with *We dropped from last year* with no meaningful follow-up for the rest of the school year, teachers and administrators in a low-performing school are left feeling like deer in the headlights: They feel powerless.

One of the most powerful forms of achievement evidence to assist schools in inventing systems for instructional change is found in teacher-driven common formative and summative assessments aligned with agreed-upon learning targets. This topic is discussed further in the section on structured learning teams in a low-performing school in *Powerless to Powerful: School Systems Change*.

Contextual Evidence

Contextual evidence is often discussed informally, but it is rarely used intentionally in answering a line of inquiry. Contextual evidence examines *necessary* background information about events, programs, and services within the school and community related to the problem of practice being examined. Discipline information, types of parent programs, before- and after-school programs to support student learning, and schoolwide systems that support academic, behavioral, and social-emotional needs are all forms of contextual evidence.

This background information is critical for a leader to have and make use of in efforts to be intentional in making sense of and aligning the work being done in the school and in the community. School staff are amazed by the number of programs a school will institute to support students—without aligning or integrating them with a specific plan. Thus most low-performing schools are activity driven and not necessarily goal driven.

Contextual evidence assists stakeholders in being more intentional regarding how programs are developed and integrated. The issue isn't necessarily resources; some schools find that the state and the district consistently provide them with money so they can invent new and innovative programs to support student learning; yet they continue to struggle. The goal is to intentionally use contextual evidence to inform decision making in developing *schoolwide systems rather than activity-driven programs.*

Demographic Evidence

Demographic evidence provides important details that allow staff to know and understand the nature of those whom they serve. Demographic evidence such as school enrollment trends, ethnicity, gender, attendance, dropout rates, language proficiency, economics, and so forth gives insight (not excuses) about how to align resources based on needs with appropriate services/programs (contextual evidence), as well as types of knowledge and training that staff will need to better deliver these services/programs.

Again, schools have an abundance of demographic evidence—the issue here is to ensure that this data is synthesized and communicated to staff on a regular basis and in a meaningful format so that it's in front of people, enabling them to apply this understanding as they problem solve and develop schoolwide systems of support.

Perceptual Evidence

The use of perceptual evidence is perhaps the most powerful pivot point for creating rapid change in a school that perceives itself as powerless. An abundance of both formal and informal perceptual data is available to the schools. Formal perceptual evidence includes surveys on topics such as climate, parent, staff, and students. The list goes on of types of surveys and focus groups that can be (and probably have been) conducted in any school, after which the results are reported to stakeholders and the school board.

Also consider informal perceptual evidence, such as the one-on-ones discussed in Lesson #1. Other forms of informal perceptual evidence become available in real-time discussions between staff and with students, parents, and community members. Perceptual evidence may take on its own life. Public opinion about whether a school is "good" or "bad" is grounded in perceptual data and is influenced by the other forms of evidence discussed.

Often districts and schools try to influence perceptual evidence with fact sheets and media blitzes about the good things they're doing to help students learn; but as was mentioned in Lesson #1, the quickest way to change perceptions of others is to try new behaviors. Formal and informal perceptual evidence give the necessary information about what behaviors need to change, in addition to providing ongoing formative feedback regarding the 45-day plan (Lesson #2) and action team results (Lesson #4).

When identifying evidence for use in improvement efforts, keep it simple. Less is certainly more. Teachers are asked to use evidence in their decision-making processes. The question is, which evidence? Leaders must do the same in creating a culture for learning and purposefully answer the question of what evidence to use in the change process.

In dysfunctional schools, staff are accustomed to data dumping: Large quantities of all forms of data are put on the table without any sense-making context or analysis being provided. Or, on the other extreme, data is briefly reviewed and then put aside for a year as business continues as usual.

When staff are asked to sift through mountains of schoolwide data, valuable time is taken away from analyzing their classroom evidence to improve instruction and learning. Schoolwide evidence needs to be analyzed carefully by the leadership team, categorized into major themes, and *then* presented to staff and community in its clearest form. Be sure to establish clear protocols to assist in understanding what the evidence says at the leadership level.

Evidence sharing is most powerful in the context of a clear question or problem of practice and when only relevant information is provided, in an organized manner, to answer that question. Initially, the question the leadership team asks to analyze the evidence is: "Which evidence provides us with information to support, create, or improve schoolwide systems that promote teaching and learning?" The conversation will most likely center on evidence that puts a spotlight on behavior management issues, academic achievement, and social-emotional concerns of students.

Evidence must be triangulated if wise decisions are to be made. To ensure that a problem of practice is addressed with reliability and understanding, analyze more than one data set and type. *Evidence is best used not to defend, but to understand the question or problem of practice being analyzed.* Evidence is the starting point to ensure that the spotlight is on the right problem and that people are not running down a rabbit hole.

Often in a school that feels powerless, leaders find they are reacting to one data set point and not taking into account other evidence that may be helpful in shedding the right amount of light on the right problem. For example: Reading scores are down—what should we do? To answer this question, the school may use only achievement evidence and then jump to conclusions about what should be done. This form of brainstorming usually leads to *best ideas* thinking instead of *best practice*.

The intentional use of all forms of selected data—contextual, perceptual, and demographic—is helpful in figuring out what to do. The key is in knowing which aspects of each type of evidence are needed to ensure that resources are used wisely. The role of leadership is to discern what evidence is most powerful before putting it in front of staff and stakeholders to use in arriving at sound decisions.

This does not mean that data should be manipulated or hidden so that leaders can sell a message to the staff or district office. If necessary, an action team can be formed to ensure that the team is interpreting the data correctly. Perceptual evidence is key in this process.

Leaders shirk their responsibilities of effective planning and leading when they dump data onto staff and community members. This wastes people's time. The expectations placed on teachers to use evidence to develop positively impactful classroom strategies and interventions are the same expectations formal leaders must meet in developing and implementing schoolwide systems that support teaching and learning. Helping leaders develop lesson plans for success in their schools through their 45-day plan and effective action teams begins with the *wise and intentional* use of evidence.

Basic Leadership Strategies

1. Divide up all schoolwide evidence—conceptual, achievement, perceptual, and demographic—among the leadership team. Have each person take an assigned area and create a document that provides the essence of what the evidence implies as it pertains to supporting teaching and learning at the schoolwide level.

   Remember—less is more. What is it that your leadership team needs to know to inform your work grounded in the 45-day plan and the related action teams? If you cannot condense the evidence for each area so that it fits on one or two pages, you have too much data. *Don't overthink it.*

2. When discussing evidence as a team, it's easy to start saying, "We need to get teachers to be better at x, y, and z—and then this problem will go away." The fingers will begin to point at the classroom in terms of curriculum, instruction, and assessment practices. There

may be some merit to this attribution of blame, but hold off on these ideas nevertheless.

At this point, the evidence is being analyzed to inform you as a leader about what you might do differently in creating schoolwide systems that support teachers and students. It's about putting the spotlight on how the school might operate differently. The key here is to analyze the school before expecting different behaviors to emerge in departments and grade levels, and from individual teachers.

3. Sort the evidence through the lenses of themes and the 45-day plan. Again, the most prevalent themes will be grounded in behavior management issues, levels of achievement systems, and social-emotional needs of students. What programs and processes are already in place or are needed to address what the evidence says *teachers and students* require?

4. As the team makes sense of evidence, begin sharing how the school should move forward. Sit down for one-on-ones with counselors, coaches, and specialists, and then with the staff. Use the protocols relating to a problem of practice described in Leadership Lessons #1 and #4. Begin discussing the current reality, how the ideal looks, and whether the evidence informs the work.

In schools that feel powerless, there are often massive system errors. These include:
   a. **Schoolwide behavioral systems,** where teachers perceive students as being out of control;
   b. **Achievement systems,** with the vast majority of students operating below expectation and receiving little or no intentional schoolwide interventions other than traditional special education or Title 1 programs; and
   c. **Social-emotional systems,** where many students are not having their basic needs met. Students may be struggling with pregnancy, homelessness, mental health challenges, or drug/alcohol issues.

Allow informal discussions to influence thinking about how the evidence is or should be informing the planning process.

5. Basing your work on the staff's informal input, focus on themes identified to ensure that you are going in the right direction. Again, *keep it simple*. How does each form of evidence and staff input inform the leadership team about where to start in systems correction and implementation?

It's tempting at this point to begin shopping for programs. One of the worst programmatic decisions a leader can make is to implement a specific program, hoping that it will fix the problem, before staff members have had a chance to make sense of the problem. The use of evidence helps stakeholders make sense of the work, identify what needs to be done, and then begin to answer the question "What can we do differently to do business in an intentional and holistic manner?"

6. Don't overthink the use of evidence—evidence should result in a call for action. As you shape your plan of action, involve those who will be directly affected by the decision. This type of involvement is the most powerful form of capacity building. It sends a message that says, "As a leader, I believe in you and your ideas."

The action teams play a key role of informing staff one-on-one, in small and large groups, of the changes desired; they also gather more information to ensure that they got it right. The action team is then modeling in their behaviors with their colleagues what leaders are modeling in their work daily around the problem-solving process.

Everyone's capacity to solve problems grows as a result of using evidence correctly—that is, using evidence to answer well-thought-out questions and ideas for improvement that support the 45-day plan. The action team (Lesson #4) is responsible for the development of the plan, and the lead administrator working with the action team is accountable for ensuring that the plan unfolds as it should.

Remember, action teams are short-lived—typically less than two weeks. Action teams are about working together more intentionally in the direction in which the evidence suggests the school should move. To build trust and confidence, the leadership team needs to allow the staff to see them *trying* new behaviors related to how business is done in the school and grounded in the evidence that informs the decisions and the progress being made.

7. Once the evidence has been identified, organized, and made sense of to drive decisions in developing and implementing systems, the scorecard has already been developed. Evidence is not helpful and cannot describe whether a school is winning or losing unless leaders are keeping score. For example, changes that are made to improve schoolwide behaviors cannot be analyzed for their success unless types of discipline referrals are tracked.

Lesson #5 states that *evidence is everything but not anything*. Evidence is everywhere. Every time a leader engages in a discussion, perceptual data is being collected.

When a formal leader investigates contextual, achievement, or demographic evidence, it's easy for that leader to jump to conclusions about what course of action to pursue. Evidence influences what we think and what we look for. Evidence can cause us to wear blinders or open our eyes to new possibilities.

The leadership team, together with staff and community members, must discern how to use the evidence wisely. People unintentionally use evidence to form coalitions and persuade others to make decisions that are most beneficial to their way of thinking. Using evidence to inform and keep score regarding the 45-day plan and the related action team will keep the school moving toward true north.

Relentless, daily collection of formal and informal evidence allows the leadership team to self-correct in regard to what is important: ensuring that systems are running smoothly in developing a culture for learning. Leaders must take time to make sense of the evidence as they ask others what it says to them.

It is the leadership team that lights the fuse for change through the use of evidence and facing the current reality—but it is collective wisdom that creates energy to move the school toward the ideal.

The wise use of evidence ensures that the right questions are being asked and that the spotlight is on the right problem. Language—the words that the leadership team uses to describe the 45-day plan—provides an opportunity for staff to know that what they have to say is important and will *influence* the direction of the school. This leads us to Leadership Lesson #6 on the power of language.

LEADERSHIP LESSON # 6:
IF TIME IS GOLDEN, THEN LANGUAGE IS PLATINUM

Use language to make your thinking visible and shape how you see and portray the world. Language is a powerful tool that can move leaders and others forward to a new ideal, or imprison them in their current reality. Every school has its own language.

The old adage *Sticks and stones will break my bones but words will never hurt me* is simply not true. Bones typically heal stronger than they were before the injury, but words last forever. Words can be a cancer that slowly eats to the core, or words can build up people and their beliefs in their capacity. In a school where stakeholders feel powerless, new words need to be invented intentionally that describe the nature of the work and how the work connects to the vision of the school.

The importance of language and how we talk about each other is widely recognized as a factor in creating a culture for learning, but it is typically mentioned and then quickly forgotten, passed over in favor of more concrete elements such as instructional practices or assessment data. It is not enough to simply recognize that language is important in creating a culture for learning within a school; it must be something that is purposefully developed and given consistent attention.

Words let you make your thinking visible to others, and therefore allow you to influence others, positively or negatively. What we say about each other and our school is the foundation in creating a school culture. Our language offers others their first opportunity to learn what we value and expect.

Carol Dweck, in her 2006 book *Mindset,* explains the importance of language in shaping students' thinking and perceptions. She argues that it is imperative for teachers to consistently communicate that they hold growth mindsets, and equally important that formal leaders communicate a growth mindset toward teachers. It is critical that informal or formal leaders model the importance of language and refuse to allow others to slip toward negative ranting. One school moving toward transformation decided to have a no-tolerance policy regarding the leadership team speaking negatively about the teachers.

In many schools that express a sense of powerlessness, it's dismaying to hear how the leadership team discusses people's capacities. *If only we didn't have this teacher . . . If only teachers would . . .* This negativity permeates the thinking of the leadership team, who clearly believe that many of the staff don't have the ability to implement the changes that are necessary.

In addition, language regarding the district office is often negative. A common sentiment is: "If only the district office would offer more support, and provide programs and systems that worked—*then* we could really do our work."

These conversations do little more than provide leaders with excuses for the school's lack of success. It is always dangerous when people build their esteem at the expense of others (Covey, 1989). Baseball teams always have a bottom of their lineup. You can fire the seventh, eighth, and ninth batters, but you'll always have a seventh, eighth, and ninth batter. The great coaches build up the bottom end of their orders to win games.

As a saying goes, "Treat people as they are, and they will remain the same. Treat people as you want them to be, and they will change." This change begins with what Covey (1989) would call proactive language.

Leadership teams must become aware of how these conversations influence the quality of their interactions with staff. When enough attention is paid to language, it will become apparent that the language needs to change (*new behavior*) if new beliefs are to be formulated about the staff and the school, which is what will allow the school to move forward.

Logan, King, and Fischer-Wright (2011) note that language can be used both diagnostically and formatively. They explain that within a culture, "there is a specific 'fingerprint' made up of language that people use" coupled with "observable behavior toward others"—and that these two elements almost invariably match, resulting in a common mood (p. 11).

In other words, language can be used to assess the state of a culture *and* to shape it. Logan et al. argue that each culture has its own theme "that appears whenever people talk, email, joke around, or just pass one another in the hallway" (p. 9). Further, they claim to be able to predict how a given culture or tribe will perform by counting how many of its members speak a common language and observing which persons hold positions of leadership (p. 14).

As time passes, note Logan et al., "the language a person speaks and . . . [the cultural stage that person is in] sync up" (p. 14). Thus, although assessment data, achievement scores, and perceptual data help educators diagnose the health of their schools, making a consistent effort to intentionally examine the language in the school will provide additional evidence to help administrators evaluate and shape the culture for learning within the school.

The right language communicates new beliefs in each person's ability to do the work. It also conveys a message regarding the vision of the school and the nature of the work of leaders in relating to that vision. Leadership teams can craft words and phrases to use intentionally to describe the work. Examples include such phrases as: *Together we will; one vision, one voice; believe and achieve; passion, persistence, patience; stop the bleeding;* and *our kids are not zeroes.* Again, the power of such language to clarify goals and bind a school together cannot be overestimated.

Healthy language development takes place at three levels. The first level is developed through one-on-ones with staff. The second level is with the group—as in professional learning communities, faculty meetings, and action teams. Finally, there is schoolwide informal language that describes the overall health of the school. Strategies will be outlined at the individual and the schoolwide levels—and when these strategies are firmly in place and modeled by the leadership team, a shift will take place at the group level.

Basic Leadership Strategies

Individual

1. Have each administrator on the leadership team take a moment to reflect on each staff person he or she is assigned to evaluate. Have each leader write specific *strengths* and *interests* that his or her assigned people have in contributing to the well-being of their students and the school.

Also take time to identify the *needs* that each person has brought
forth in discussions about improving his or her classrooms or school.
A guiding question is, "If you googled that person's name, what
would pop up?" This is called the SIN principle—working toward
Strengths, Interests, and Needs. It is important for formal leaders to
SIN in all that they do when working with those whom they serve.

2. Then let each leader share with the team the words he or she used to
   describe each of the relevant staff person's strengths, interests, and
   needs. Ask colleagues whether they agree with the narrative.

3. In one-on-ones, listen deeply to assigned staff persons to learn what
   they are proud of in their accomplishments, in the classrooms, with
   their students, or in their schoolwide efforts. Find out what each
   person is excited about. Also listen for their perceived needs. See
   whether the written catalog from Step 2 aligns with observations
   based on the new information.

4. Agree on a new leadership team meeting norm, for example: *No
   leader may talk negatively about a staff person or the staff as whole during
   a leadership team meeting.* Phrases such as "If only they would . . . ,"
   "He needs to learn . . . ," and the like are not allowed.

   Acknowledge that if staff aren't living up to expectations, that
   deficit says more about leaders than about the staff. Focus on where
   staff need to be led, as a group or an individual, in moving toward a
   new ideal, and on the behaviors or methods of communication leaders need to demonstrate.

   If a leader is having difficulty with a specific staff person, that is a
   management issue to be discussed at the end of the leadership team
   meeting. Address each situation on an individual basis, not according to a preconceived paradigm.

   Discuss specific strategies for reconnecting that staff person to the
   well-being of the school. Emphasize the individual's unmet needs
   and specific supports that can be developed to help him or her succeed. Rehearse difficult conversations with each other before going
   to the identified person to create *problem-solving* opportunities with
   the staff person rather than *power-over* conversations. Often one or
   two troubled staff members can dominate a discussion, making decisions for the whole group instead of focusing on the problem.

5. Provide specific feedback *daily* to each assigned staff person on the
   actions she or he is taking that support the vision of the school. Recognize each person's self-perceived strengths in a way that lets the individual know that these strengths are valued and how these strengths
   help staff and students and promote the vision of the school.

6. Catch people doing things right as the schoolwide initiatives are
   developed and implemented. As new processes and systems are

refined or invented, continually point out to each person how she or he is necessary to the success of positive changes and point out what she or he is doing to help make it happen. This affirmation builds both efficacy and capacity.

Schoolwide

1. As a leadership team, discuss the significance of each of the over-arching goals of the 45-day plan. What does success look like, and what words would describe that success?
2. Invent a very short phrase or slogan that best describes the mission of the school. One school chose *Together we will* for the first year, which then became the stem for future slogans. Year two was *Together we will believe and achieve,* and year three became *Together we will exceed expectations.* As the leadership team became clearer in their expectations, they also got better at inventing language to describe their work.
3. Be intentional in using the same words that describe the ideal in one-on-ones and in small groups.
4. Invite students and staff to invent phrases that describe collective efforts to support and improve teaching and learning.
5. Invent language to describe the nature of the work. Use such language openly with each other and in front of the staff; this creates a sense of accountability and transparency. Examples of words that can be used include:
   a. "Tend our gardens"—the area of focus within the 45-day plan for which each leader is responsible and accountable.
   b. "Guardian angel"—the person assigned to either staff or students to ensure success—a mentor, colleague, parent—an advocate across services.
   c. "Audit"—a quick reality check to see whether the intended outcome is the actual outcome.
   d. "Skin in the game"—everyone having some level of responsibility or accountability for what is being implemented.
   e. "The Big Three"—the notions of (1) envisioning the future, (2) having everyone connected to the school in a meaningful way, and (3) creating powerful relationships.
   f. "Academic press, social support, and relational trust"—elements of the conceptual framework that are openly discussed, defined, and regularly analyzed by everyone on staff.

Such phrases remind everyone of what is important. They tend to catch on very quickly at all levels of the school, with both students and staff. Over time, the language in the school becomes healthy at both the individual and the schoolwide levels. The language defines leadership's thinking, and leadership's thinking defines the language.

Staff and students then begin to focus on possibilities rather than deficits. An abundance mentality (Covey, 1989) begins to emerge as people no longer fear a scarcity of resources, either internal or external. People believe in each other and that problems can be seen as opportunities for success. Additionally, the common language provides a school with a kind of shorthand, meaning people can communicate easily about complex topics.

The importance of developing intentional language cannot be overstated. John Wooden, the famous UCLA basketball coach, won ten NCAA national championships; at one point his team won eighty-eight games in a row. He was observed for several days to discern what he did to achieve such results. What the observers realized was that Coach Wooden spent 10 percent of his time giving new information, 85 percent providing specific feedback and praise regarding what his players were doing in moving toward the desired behavior or outcome, and 5 percent of his time offering corrective feedback.

This is a powerful model for a leadership team. The team can use specific language with each person, describing to each individual his or her strengths, interests, and needs. In one-on-ones, specific language is used to "catch" each person doing things right every day—behaviors that foster the vision of the school. The leadership team thus discovers and manifests the power of developing one-on-ones and schoolwide language that connect emotion regarding the vision to the specific person.

Intentional leadership language leads to a sense of schoolwide hopefulness in that staff perceive that the leaders know where they are taking them and how each person fits into the vision. Creating new language leads to a deeper understanding of the common goals and makes leaders aware of how they may have previously failed as a team in terms of how they talked about their work publicly and privately, whether with students, staff, or the district office. Here we arrive at Lesson #7: building a relationship with the district office.

LEADERSHIP LESSON #7: DISTRICT OFFICE: FRIEND OR FOE?

Work with the district office in a way that promotes its active support in attaining the vision of the school. Remember: Pushing against the wind is wasted effort. You can control only what you can control.

When a school is failing, its employees are under a lot of pressure from a variety of sources to improve. So, too, is the district office. Federal and state officials, community members, parents, and school boards are consistently asking district personnel what they're doing with the schools that are performing poorly. Often, leadership coaches are assigned to the building principal, or new programs with intensive professional development are prescribed, with little to no buy-in from the school. The net result is a flurry of activity that includes moving principals around and bringing in more outside support and additional staff members in hopes of improving test scores.

Many of the feelings that teachers experience toward leadership in a low-achieving school are the same feelings that principals feel toward district office personnel. The routine goes something like this: The principal goes to a district office meeting and gets his or her marching orders. Typically, these center on management issues such as budget, assessment systems, curriculum changes, and new mandates.

After the meeting, the principal goes back to the building and someone asks how it went. The response: "Oh, you know, more work to do that has nothing to do with my job." The language itself sets the stage for coalition formation and an "us versus them" mindset. Shortly thereafter, the principal calls a faculty meeting and tells the teachers about the changes in curriculum, additional reports regarding assessments, and the training that will follow the new curriculum requirements—oh, and by the way, the budget has been cut by 10 percent.

Everyone looks at everyone else in the room, and the feeling of helplessness sets in. Everyone is thinking, *How can I do all this—I'm not even prepared to make it through tomorrow.* All the while the principal puts on an unconvincing smile and says something to effect of, "You're a great group of dedicated teachers and I know we'll get through all this. We know the kids are what's important here. Know that the district office and I are here to help you as much as we can."

After the meeting, some of teachers continue talking in the parking lot: "All they do is put more work on us that doesn't have anything to do with our work in the classroom. If they'd just leave us alone to teach, those test scores would go up." This is another *if only* statement that contributes to coalition formation, reinforcing a feeling of "us against them." If this is how the *teachers* are feeling, it's unlikely that the support staff, students, and parents are feeling empowered.

In a school where people feel powerless, leaders don't believe all of the teachers can do the work; teachers don't believe that their leaders can do the work; and the district office doesn't believe that the school can do the work. And most don't believe the students and parents are up for the work. Often people don't know exactly how to do their work, so they point fingers at each other and say, "This is what you need to do differently and things will improve."

In reality, the best question in becoming powerful is: *How do we support each other in different ways in order to **act** and make sense of how to do our work?* If everyone *knew* how to do the work, then all schools would be exceeding expectations.

As discussed, effective leaders are able to frame in the problem with supporting evidence. They put structures in place for people to engage in the problem-solving process, develop meaningful leadership plans, and then act intentionally toward the desired outcome through systems at all levels of the schoolhouse.

There's no doubt that those in the district office need to transform how they help building leaders in a low-achieving school. Honig et al. (2010, preface) tried to answer this question: "What does it take for leaders to promote and support powerful, equitable learning in a school and in the district and state system that serves the school?" They found that effective district office practices included developing partnerships with school leaders that built capacity throughout educational systems for teaching and learning improvements.

A key element of district office transformation is helping principals become learning leaders. The change is based not on providing external supports, but rather on *focusing the district office on their commitment to doing the work with the building.* This is related to the concept of building leaders working with their staff to focus them on doing the right work. Relationships, problem solving, capacity building, and systems integration are key at both the district and the school levels in leadership transformation.

If indeed this is a partnership between the district office and the building, then what are the behaviors a building leader needs to be able to demonstrate to the district office to elicit their support? It's easy to describe what the district needs to do from the perspective of the building, and to describe what the building needs to do from the perspective of the district office.

Covey (1989) describes the concepts of "circle of concern" and "span of control." Circles of concern are things a person worries about but doesn't have control over, such as the budget, and state and federal laws. Span of control includes things a person has direct control over, such as 45-day plans that support teaching and learning, budgets that align resources with grade level/departmental needs and schoolwide systems, the nature of conversations in one-on-ones, or what a person declares she or he is accountable for accomplishing.

Covey stated that if you stay within your span of control, you increase your effectiveness and your circle of concern will diminish. The feeling of being overwhelmed that besets building leaders and staff stems from perceiving that what *they have to do* is outside of their span of control; that feeling falls within the circle of concern. Living in the circle of concern leads to worry, fear, and a sense of helplessness.

Effective leaders don't just make considerations within their span of control—they also *act* within their span of control. Taking charge of what can be focused on and sharing problems in an intentional way with the district office is the first step in developing a partnership. A building leader must have the capacity and support to establish:

- a collective vision;
- a plan;
- systems to support the plan; and
- structures to support ongoing problem solving so that the school can self-correct when it is not moving toward its defined ideal.

How can a school expect help from the district office if the building leader isn't informing district office personnel about the plan and related systems in ways that allow the district office to engage with the school in the change process? Share the problem in a way that others can hear, and collective action will be more likely to follow. If leaders believe that the district office is a foe, then it is; and if they believe it is a friend—then this is true as well.

Basic Leadership Strategies

1. In leadership team meetings, begin to ask questions about how the district office might help in the implementation of that 45-day plan. Overcommunicate with the district office regarding the goals of the plan and systems under construction. Stay away from the natural instinct of asking for more resources and for the district office to provide *external support* in realizing the ideal. Initially, it's not about more resources; it's about *ownership, capacity building,* and *rethinking how business is done*. It's about *developing a culture for learning*.
2. Challenge the system. Kouzes and Posner (2012) discuss the importance of leaders' not being afraid to shake things up. Leaders who challenge the system are not afraid to confront obstacles, and they refuse to accept the status quo. Leaders who challenge the system take on risks, knowing that mistakes will be made along the way. Mistakes are seen as opportunities to learn.

   In a school that feels powerless, the status quo cannot be accepted. The building leader of a low-performing school must challenge the system at all levels. It's important that the building leader challenge the system, especially in regard to management decisions that are barriers to achieving the ideal that *appear* to come from the district office—decisions about budget, staffing allocation, special education rules, district assessment requirements, and beyond.

The more the leader knows, the more powerful that leader becomes in terms of thinking about and using resources in creative and flexible ways to support the 45-day plan.

3. Take this newfound knowledge as the beginning of thinking outside the box regarding how to align resources with building needs that support program and system development. Principals are likely to hear variations on these themes: "We can't do it that way because the law doesn't allow us to—it won't pass muster in an audit," or "This isn't how we do it in this district." Often these are well-intentioned but uninformed knee-jerk responses, grounded in how the responder interpreted the rules, was trained to do the work, or feels a need to play it safe. The district office's responses reflect its perception of current reality.

   Don't accept no for an answer. When building leaders hear "No!" from the district office, they need to do their homework and call the people outside of the district who are informed. Many rules and regulations turn out to be flexible when the programs are known and the intent of the policy is understood and acknowledged. Often, the disconnect between buildings such as the school and the district office is found in the procedure, not the policy, and that's what the leader challenges.

4. Encourage the person at the district level to join the problem-solving process and to think outside the box. Assure the individual that you honor the policy, which likely describes an ideal, but note that you question the procedures assigned to achieve it. Envision together the possibilities through asking *What if . . . In a perfect world . . . Are there alternatives?*

   Leaders who believe they have a way that is better than the prescribed mandate need to propose the alternative and show how it meets the *district needs/policies,* fosters *building goals,* and addresses the *intent of the policy.* As always, they do well to look for common ground.

5. Remember, district office personnel want every building to be successful. They are not the enemy.

In most cases, the district office is an important advocate in the change process. If there's an absence of vision and an apparent leadership void, then external factors will fill that void by developing policy and practices for leaders at the building level. Leaders must have faith in their gut—supported by data, a plan, and articulated processes and systems that support the work of quality teaching and students' learning.

Don't be afraid to lead. A leader needs to be able to articulate where she or he is taking the building, align resources in a way that supports the vision, and have clear processes and structures in place to engage the staff in the work. If a leader is able to describe the work clearly to key district office personnel, support will follow. If the district office is the fuel that provides the vision through policy and work with formal leaders, then the support staff in the building are the glue that holds the team together. This brings us to our final lesson.

LEADERSHIP LESSON #8:
SUPPORT THE ONES WHO SUPPORT THE WORK

Listen to and act on the words of wisdom of the support staff. They have an important lens on the school, especially in terms of how others perceive it. Be sure that support staff are actively involved in the change process in a way that builds their capacity and ensures that they are able to communicate to others in a trustworthy manner.

Sources that community members and parents trust most to give them accurate information about the school include students, support staff (e.g., custodians, secretaries, teacher aides, cooks, bus drivers), certificated staff, building level administrators, and finally, district office officials (Decker & Decker, 2003). Support staff act as a valuable link; they provide an understanding about what is happening in the school to outside stakeholders; yet often they are last to be intentionally communicated with by formal leaders within the school.

People outside the school who are not "in the know" trust what support staff say about the quality of the school. At the same time, formal leaders often believe that the information shared by the support staff can be partial and misleading. Information for support staff too often comes solely from what they observe.

Know that support staff are formulating opinions about the quality of the school based on what they see students, teachers, and administrators say and do. Support staff's opinions and beliefs about the quality of the school will make or break a struggling school's opportunity to *regain* trust with parents and community members.

In a hurting school, support staff often feel like the last people in the pecking order and are underappreciated. This dearth of acknowledgment results in ill will and the feeling of being "done to." Support staff at these schools often make comments that suggest they feel powerless:

- "I do my job and go home."
- "I never know what's going on around here."

- "If anybody asked me, I could tell them how to run this school."
- "Nobody cares about or appreciates what I think and do."
- "They sure make a lot of money and expect *me* to do *their* work."

These staff members have knowledge, but are given no arena in which to apply it.

If certificated staff are feeling mistreated and misunderstood by administrators, then support staff are likely to have those feelings about their treatment at the hands of both administrators *and* certificated staff. Often support staff are an army of one or two in their job assignments and feel very much alone.

When support staff talk with each other, they typically have a lot to say about how they perceive the effectiveness of specific certificated staff and administrators, and about the school climate. In turning around a school that feels powerless, it's wise to put a special light on the support staff in a way that promotes *two-way* communication. This communication allows formal leaders to gain an important lens on the health of the school.

Many of the strategies discussed in the previous Lessons Learned apply when working with support staff, but they may play out differently. When doing one-on-ones or developing the 45-day plan, formal leaders must be intentional in communicating often and effectively with support staff, and they must make sure that support staff are engaged in the planning process.

Support staff need to be believed in by formal leaders and certificated staff in a way that builds their capacity to do the work. Support staff are instrumental in the turnaround process. Often they're waiting eagerly to be invited to help with the turnaround efforts of the school.

The skill set and strategies needed for working with each type of support staff are much like those necessary for working with the certificated staff. That said, let's turn to a discussion of the three most frequently forgotten support staff, those who are often not *intentionally and collectively* communicated with on an ongoing basis by formal leadership: building secretaries, custodians, and food service workers.

Building Secretaries

Building secretaries are the eyes and ears of the principal as well as the face of the school. Ongoing *informal and formal* communication must take place between the leaders of the school and the secretaries. The *lead* secretary in the main office plays a unique role in the communication process and must be *aware of everything the principal is thinking and doing* to create change in the school.

1. Meet formally with the lead secretary on a weekly basis, either before or after school. These meetings are critical and are a time to discuss both management and leadership issues. Listen deeply to the secretary's concerns about being in the loop regarding such items as the calendar, events in the building, the budget, building cleanliness, when staff are in and out of the building, and more.

   When secretaries cannot communicate basic information with staff, parents, and community members, they feel disconnected and unable to do their jobs well. A secretary should never have to respond to a stakeholder's question with "I don't know. They never tell me what's going on around here." *Empower your secretarial team to make decisions and act on the information provided.*

   Know that mistakes will be made along the way, but as different situations arise and are discussed, capacity is built in basic decision-making. That will free the leadership team to be visible in the school.

2. Share important leadership issues that center on the 45-day plan. When it's appropriate, be sure to invite the lead secretary to the planning sessions. Take time to listen to the secretary's ideas and concerns about the plan.

3. Take time during the weekly meeting with the lead secretary to ask questions about what he or she hears staff saying. What are staff talking about in the office? What are the secretary's perceptions concerning the pulse of the school? Is there something the administration can do better in communicating with and supporting all staff? Discern the perceived "hot spots" and the overall health of the school. Integrate new thinking into your behaviors when working with staff. Also, share your frustrations and concerns openly.

4. Each day, conduct one-on-ones with all secretaries about administrative issues, and do a reality check on the climate of the day and whether there's a need for any follow-up with specific staff. Do routine audits to analyze whether the lead secretary is communicating effectively.

5. Model and develop your lead secretary's capacity to be the lead facilitator of a secretaries' professional learning community. Be sure to give secretaries time to meet weekly in their PLCs to discuss schedules, clarify roles and responsibilities, and find ways to support each other in their work.

   The secretaries are the first ones to greet the customers, and the more they know, the better they can communicate timely and accurate information. Encourage secretaries to work together to find ways to communicate better, provide training for each other, and develop specific targets for improvement. They can write a team purpose statement, develop group norms, outline related goals, and affirm role responsibilities.

The principal may find that it is important to take them through this process so that each secretary, regardless of his or her department, is clearly an extension of the main office and cannot be seen as a separate entity. The principal must provide clear expectations and empower the secretaries to do their work. The lead secretary is *accountable* for the management of all the school offices, and each secretary has important responsibilities for specific operations of the school, which must be viewed as a collective whole.

6. Give secretaries an opportunity to come up with a purpose statement. It may be something like: "The purpose of the [name of school] secretarial staff is to provide a culture of support and to communicate accurate information to all stakeholders in a professional and courteous manner." All of their goals must grow from the agreed-upon purpose.

7. Meet routinely with the secretaries' PLC to answer questions, engage in problem solving, and continually emphasize that no single department functions independently. The big idea is that the more they understand what's going on in the school, the better everyone can support each other and grow in capacity.

8. Learn from silence. If the office isn't a hub of friendly chatter throughout the school day, that may tell you something about the climate.

Building Custodians

Like secretaries, building custodians have a unique understanding of hot spots in a school. They are very much aware of the dynamics between staff and students in given classrooms or portions of the building. Custodians are able to tell which teachers let students off the hook on schoolwide expectations or have poor classroom management. Custodians know when staff and students are having a bad day by the overall cleanliness of the school.

The custodial staff's communication to the outside world tells a story to the community about whether there is personal pride in the school. In a school that's struggling, ask the custodian about the cleanliness of the school after high-stakes testing week, after report cards have been issued, or around specific holidays such as Christmas or Thanksgiving. The cleanliness of the school and grounds is a direct reflection of the climate of the school and provides feedback to staff and administration regarding whether students have pride in their school and how they feel about how adults there treat them.

1. Do bimonthly *walkabouts* of the building and grounds with lead custodians, including one with their district supervisor. Listen intently to the day custodians' thoughts about what the hot spots are and what assistance they need from staff, students, and the district office in keeping the building clean. Also, be clear when sharing expectations.

2. Develop a system so that the lead custodian works with the student leadership team. Listen to the students' thoughts about their role in keeping the school clean and establish collaborative goals. Students must feel that roles and expectations are developed *with* them and not *for* them.

3. Devise a way to keep score. Have routine walkabouts with student leaders and custodians to provide feedback about whether cleanliness goals are being met. Have students communicate with other students verbally and visually regarding the goals and progress being made in achieving these goals. Continually update staff on these goals and their expected support roles.

4. Meet once a month with the day and night crew together. Listen to their concerns and address their needs. Be sure the building schedule is clear so that there are no surprises regarding activities that are going on and the related contact people. Make sure the crew has the tools they need to do their work.

Openly share your 45-day plan and your perception that custodians play an important role in the turnaround process. Demonstrate in both words and actions that their work is valued. Remind them that the first image for community stakeholders concerns the cleanliness of the school and the use of their tax dollars.

This commitment from formal leaders to helping custodians to do their work will build capacity and personal pride. A sense of increased ownership on the part of staff and students regarding the cleanliness of their school will be clearly communicated to the community by the custodians and will be one of the first areas in which stakeholders will begin to see that something positive is happening in the school.

Food Services

Cooks and food servers have a unique lens on students and the culture of the school. They are privy to in-line chatter and are well aware of the needs of the most at-risk students. They also gain inside information about how the students are feeling about their school. Food service workers are often caring people who are concerned about the health of the students.

Furthermore, food quality and type are important to the students. Lunchtime can either enhance the culture of the school or bring it down. Are students in the lunch line viewed as cattle being herded through the food lines, or is lunchtime seen as a chance to break bread together and have an enjoyable experience? Lunchtime can be a useful tool in developing a culture for learning and providing a safe haven for students— especially in a school that is trying to regain a sense of power.

Basic Leadership Strategies

1. Be clear on the vision that the lunchroom is a place to enhance the culture of the school, a culture in which people respect each other and play together in a caring way. Involve food service workers and students working together in establishing the purpose and goals of lunchtime. The lunchroom should not just be a place to rush through the line and get food, but a place to receive nourishment together, share, and talk.

   What food do people want? What kind of atmosphere would be most constructive? How can students be a part of supporting a positive environment? In their discussions, have students and food service personnel share what's going well and what is not working. Make sure the conversation is open and candid and takes place on a regular basis; twice a month works well. Topics for these meetings can include:

   a. Developing a lunchroom that is joyful and student centered, one that fosters a relaxed atmosphere. Give students a sense of autonomy; let them decorate the lunch area in a way that provides reminders for all students about what being successful looks like. Emphasize manners, manners, manners. Teach students and staff to say "please" and "thank you" as they pass through the lines.

   b. Identifying ways in which students can be involved in planning the menu for the school. This is the time for food service workers to educate students about the requirements put forth by the federal government regarding a nutritious lunch.

   c. Planning formal events with the students and food services personnel. Such events include having formal sit-down lunches with special foods for holidays served by school staff—and allowing food services workers to be served by students. Make events festive by having students and staff dress up and eat together; and provide special recognition for support staff, district office personnel, and other stakeholders during these special events.

2. Meet with food services personnel monthly to identify hot spots. Take time to hear about students who may have special needs or

challenges, or other issues that students have shared with personnel. Be open about where the school is going and how food services fits into the overall well-being of the school.

Lunchtime can either escalate the problems of the school or provide a time to rejuvenate staff and students for the rest of the day. Too often formal leaders busy themselves with duties during lunchtime, rather than taking that time to create lunchrooms that foster relationship building among students as well as between students and staff.

Support staff are more likely to represent the demographic profile and the culture of the community than are the certificated and formal leaders of the school. Take time to listen to and understand what they are saying about the school, because their thinking aligns with and will influence community perceptions of the school.

Often support staff hear platitudes such as "Oh, you're so great," "We couldn't run this school without you," or "You're the best!" If these things are true, then empower them to do their work. Listen to them and build their capacity by involving them in problem solving and acting on ideas that support the vision of the work.

Engaging support staff to do the work in an intentional way with students and staff makes them part of the change process and the 45-day plan. Knowledge is power. Letting the support staff in on the secret of where you're taking them (that is, if you know where you're taking them) and the help you need from them in getting there will be an eye-opening experience.

Again, knowing where you're taking them begins with having a 45-day plan, listening to them, and then discussing the possibilities of where they fit in. The notion of *together we will* does spill into the community—which communicates that something special is happening in the school. Working effectively with the support staff builds a climate that is inclusive and puts in place another building block to support the turnaround process.

SUMMARY

A key element that is embedded in each of the Lessons Learned is connecting with and building the capacity of all to manifest the vision of the school. The formal leaders are the ones who light the fuse to initiate change through demonstrating new behaviors that instill new beliefs in staff and students. The real explosion occurs when these new beliefs are understood and are used to foster personal and group capacity building. The Lessons Learned are grounded in having high expectations (academic press) and systems that support others in achieving these expectations (social support). These expectations and systems are developed through two-way communication that fosters relational trust through problem-solving skills in a safe environment, and through role clarification that allows people to know each other's strengths and work collaboratively. The overarching result is that each person's skill set and strengths contribute to the well-being and vision of the school.

Formal leaders must be intentional in their two-way conversations (both in one-on-ones and in small groups) and in collecting and analyzing evidence that leads to the development of clear themes and goal clarification. In all likelihood, themes will center on *behavioral management, social-emotional needs,* and *achievement levels of students.*

Developing a clear plan and using time wisely in a way that supports the implementation of systems to address these themes are the beginning steps in supporting staff in their work and the turnaround process. Each system implemented that supports behavior management, social-emotional needs, and achievement of students is grounded in high expectations and specific help through targeted intervention programs.

Departments and grade levels will begin to take risks and examine their practices when they feel collectively supported by well-defined schoolwide systems and are engaged in the work of a professional learning community.

Ultimately, the goal is a humanistic one: to treat everyone—students, teachers, administrators, parents, support staff, and those in the district office—like distinct and valuable contributors. Each person wants to be recognized as an individual. Wise leaders take the time to honor and serve those individuals and those gifts, enhancing and promoting them to rebuild a school that feels powerless from the inside out. The result will be a school where people feel that they have choices and input. They will feel powerful, take pride and ownership, hold themselves accountable, and have increased energy and commitment to do the work they signed up to do.

Administrators will do their work differently, with a sense that they have the power to make choices. Formal leaders will listen carefully and diagnose thoughtfully to make sure that the spotlight is put on the right problem. Then purposeful action will result, and in the process, the beliefs of those who are led will be changed. The culture will shift from being based on fear to being based on vision and goals.

This book provides a framework grounded in work that has supported renewed efforts in others, but it is not a recipe for success. That idea is too prescriptive and doesn't honor the complexities inherent in a school. It is because of these complexities that understanding and committing to a conceptual framework is so important. The processes then emerge from commonly held beliefs. Systems can then be built and rebuilt in continual pursuit of true north in an ever-changing landscape.

Specific suggestions for bringing about positive changes in attitudes, beliefs, and behaviors are offered in *Powerless to Powerful: School Systems Change*. The volume discusses specific schoolwide systems, constructive ways to involve parents, and the role learning teams and 45-day plans play in guiding the work of the systems. Once these changes are implemented, a school that once felt powerless is likely to exhibit the ability to change and grow that brings about not only increased student achievement, but also a sense of belonging, being cared for, and having an important role to play among all constituents, a sense that results in a feeling of personal and organizational power.

References

Ahram, R., Stembridge, A., Fergus, E., and Noguera, P. (2001). Framing urban school challenges: The problems to examine when implementing Response to Intervention. *RTI Action Network*. Retrieved from http://www.duplinschools.net/Page/1679.

ASCD (Association for Supervision and Curriculum Development). (2004). *The learning compact redefined: A call to action*. Retrieved from http://www.ascd.org/learningcompact.

Baier, A. (1986). Trust and antitrust. *Ethics, 96*(2), 231–60. Retrieved from www.jstor.org.

Bandura, A. (1997). *Self-efficacy: The exercise of control*. New York, NY: Worth.

Benard, B. (1991). *Fostering resiliency in kids: Protective factors in the family, school, and community*. Portland, OR: Western Center for Drug-Free Schools and Communities.

Bryk, A. S., and Driscoll, M. E. (1988). *The high school as community: Contextual influences and consequences for students and teachers*. Madison: National Center on Effective Secondary Schools, University of Wisconsin–Madison.

Bryk, A., Lee, V., and Holland, P. (1993). *Catholic schools and the common good*. Cambridge, MA: Harvard University Press.

Bryk, A. S., and Schneider, B. (2003). Trust in schools: A core resource for school reform. *Educational Leadership, 60*(6), 40–5. Retrieved from http://www.ascd.org/publications/educational-leadership/mar03/vol60/num06/Trust-in-Schools@-A-Core-Resource-for-School-Reform.aspx.

Cottrell, S. (2001). *Teaching study skills and supporting learning*. Basingstoke, UK: Palgrave.

Covey, S. (1992). *Principle-centered leadership*. New York, NY: Free Press.

Covey, S. (1989). *The 7 habits of highly effective people*. New York, NY: Free Press.

Covey, S., Merrill, A. R., and Merrill, R. R. (1996). *First things first*. New York, NY: Free Press.

Decker, L. E., and Decker, V. A. (2003). *Home, school, and community partnerships*. Lanham, MD: Scarecrow Press.

Dixon, A. L., and Tucker, C. (2008). Every student matters: Enhancing strengths-based school counseling through the application of mattering. *Professional School Counseling, 12*(2), 123–6.

DuFour, R., DuFour, R., and Eaker, R. (2009). New insights into professional learning communities at work. In M. Fullan (ed.), *The challenge of change: Start school improvement now!* (2nd ed., pp. 87–104). Thousand Oaks, CA: Corwin.

DuFour, R. *Creating professional learning communities*. [PowerPoint slides]. Presentation at Washington State ASCD Annual Conference, March 6, Spokane, WA.

Durlack, J. A., Dymnicki, A. B., Taylor, R. D., Weissberg, R. P., and Schellinger, K. B. (2011). The impact of enhancing students' social and emotional learning: A meta-analysis of school-based universal interventions. *Child Development, 82*(1), 474–501. doi:10.1111/j.1467-8624.2010.01564.x.

Edeburn, S. (2010). *Students' perception of relational trust and the impact it has on their desire to learn*. (Unpublished master's thesis). Gonzaga University, Spokane, WA.

Fitch, T. J., and Marshall, J. L. (2004). What counselors do in high-achieving schools: A study on the role of the school counselor. *Professional School Counseling, 7*(3), 172–7.

Fordham University. (2013). *Fordham's Jesuit tradition*. Retrieved from http://www.fordham.edu/discover_fordham/fordhams_jesuit_trad/.

Fullan, M. (2011). *Motion leadership: The skinny on becoming change savvy*. Retrieved from http://www.michaelfullan.ca/images/handouts/11_TheSkinny_A4.pdf.

Gaines, E. (2011). *The effectiveness of the Ethics 1 Workshop on first-time bystander offenders*. (Unpublished master's thesis). Gonzaga University, Spokane, WA.

Giles, C., & Hargreaves, A. (2006). The sustainability of innovative schools as learning organizations and professional learning communities during standardized reform. *Educational Administration Quarterly, 42*(1), 124–56. doi:10.1177/0013161X05278189.

Glickman, C. D. (1990). *Supervision of instruction: A developmental approach*. Boston, MA: Allyn & Bacon.

Glickman, C. D., Gordon, S. P., and Ross-Gordon, J. M. (1998). *Supervision of instruction: A developmental approach* (4th ed.). Boston: Allyn and Bacon.

Goddard, R. D., Salloum, S., and Berebitsky, D. (2009). Trust as a mediator of the relationships between academic achievement, poverty and minority status: Evidence from Michigan's public elementary schools. *Educational Administration Quarterly, 45*(2), 292–311. doi:10.1177/0013161X08330503.

Gonzaga University. (n.d.). *Jesuit education*. Retrieved from https://www.gonzaga.edu/about/mission/Jesuit-Education.asp.

Gonzaga University. (2013). *Mission statement*. Retrieved from http://www.gonzaga.edu/about/mission/missionstatement.asp.

Greenleaf, R. K. (1970). *The servant as leader*. Indianapolis, IN: Robert K. Greenleaf Center for Servant Leadership.

Harper, B. E. (2009). "I've never seen or heard it this way!" Increasing student engagement through the use of technology-enhanced feedback. *Teaching Edu-*

cational Psychology, 3(3), 1–8. Retrieved from http://files.eric.ed.gov/fulltext/EJ829082.pdf.

Heifetz, R. A. (1998). *Leadership without easy answers.* Cambridge, MA: Harvard University Press.

Hersey, P. H., Blanchard, K. H., and Johnson, D. E. (2012). *Management of organizational behavior: Leading human resources* (10th ed.). Upper Saddle River, NJ: Prentice-Hall.

Honig, M. I., Copland, M. A., Rainey, L., Lorton, J. A., Newton, M., Matson, E.,et al. (2010, April). *Central office transformation for district-wide teaching and learning improvement.* Retrieved from http://depts.washington.edu/ctpmail/PDFs/S2-CentralAdmin-04-2010.pdf.

Hoy, W. K., Tarter, C. J., and Woolfolk Hoy, A. (2006). Academic optimism of schools: A force for student achievement. *American Education Research Journal, 43*(3), 425–46. doi:10.3102/00028312043003425.

Ingersoll, R. M. (2004). *Why do high-poverty schools have difficulty staffing their classrooms with qualified teachers?* [Report prepared for Renewing Our Schools, Preparing Our Future]. Retrieved from http://www.americanprogress.org/kf/ingersoll-final.pdf.

Krovetz, M. L. (2007). *Fostering resilience: Expecting all students to use their minds and hearts well* (2nd ed.). Thousand Oaks, CA: Corwin.

Kouzes, J. M., and Posner, B. Z. (2012). *The leadership challenge: How to make extraordinary things happen in organizations* (5th ed.). San Francisco, CA: Jossey-Bass.

Lange, C. M., and Sletten, S. J. (2002, February 1). *Alternative education: A brief history and synthesis.* Retrieved from https://www.sde.idaho.gov/site/alternative_schools/docs/alt/alternative_ed_history%202002.pdf.

Lee, V. E., and Smith, J. B. (1999). Social support and achievement for young adolescents in Chicago: The role of school academic press. *American Educational Research Journal, 36,* 907–45. doi:10.3102/00028312036004907.

Lee, V. E., Smith, J. B., Perry, T. E., and Smylie, M. A. (1999). *Social support, academic press, and student achievement: A view from the middle grades in Chicago.* Retrieved from https://ccsr.uchicago.edu/sites/default/files/publications/p0e01.pdf.

Lencioni, P. (2002). *The five dysfunctions of a team: A leadership fable.* San Francisco, CA: Jossey-Bass.

Logan, D., King, J., and Fischer-Wright, H. (2011). *Tribal leadership: Leveraging natural groups to build a thriving organization.* New York, NY: HarperBusiness. Retrieved from http://www.triballeadership.net/media/tribal_leadership_chapter _1-2.pdf-2.pdf.

Lumsden, L. (1997). *Expectations for students.* Retrieved from https://scholarsbank.uoregon.edu/xmlui/bitstream/handle/1794/3338/digest116.pdf?sequence=1.

Murphy, J. F., Weil, M., Halliger, P., and Mitman, A. (1989). Academic press: Translating high expectations into school policies and classroom practices. *Educational Leadership, 40*(30), 22–6. Retrieved from www.ascd.org/ASCD/pdf/journals/ed_lead/el_198212_murphy.pdf.

Muller, C. (2001). The role of caring in the teacher-student relationship for at-risk students. *Sociological Inquiry, 71*(2), 241–55. doi: 10.1111/j.1475-682X.2001.tb01110.x.

Mussoline, L. J., and Shouse, R. C. (2001). School restructuring as a policy agenda: Why one size may not fit all. *Sociology of Education, 74,* 44–58. doi:10.2307/2673144.

National Center for Public Policy and Higher Education and the Southern Regional Education Board. (2010, June). *Beyond the rhetoric: Improving college readiness through coherent state policy.* Retrieved from http://www.highereducation.org/reports/college_readiness/CollegeReadiness.pdf.

Natriello, G., and McDill, E. (1986). Performance standards, student effort on homework, and academic achievement. *Sociology of Education, 59,* 18–31.

NCES (National Center for Education Statistics). (1996, June). *Urban schools: The challenge of location and poverty.* L. Lippman, S. Burns, and E. McArthur. Retrieved from http://nces.ed.gov/pubs/96184all.pdf.

Newmann, F. M., and Wehlage, G. G. (1995, October). *Successful school restructuring: A report to the public and educators.* Retrieved from http://www.wcer.wisc.edu/archive/cors/Successful_School_Restruct.html.

North East School Division. (n.d.). *Principal's professional learning communities resource book.* Retrieved from Sylvania.neds.ca/files/u1/curric-PLC_Handbook_MW.doc.

Oh, D. M., Kim, J. M., and Leyva, B. A. (2004). Inner city teachers' sense of efficacy towards minority students. *Journal of Research for Educational Leaders, 2*(2), 55–78. Retrieved from http://www2.education.uiowa.edu/archives/jrel/fall04/Oh-Kim-Leyva_0410.htm.

Ormberg, T. (2013). Teacher and student perceptions of academic press and social support at Sunnyside High School. (Unpublished master's thesis).

Osher, D., Sprague, R., Weissberg, R. P., Axelrod, J., Keenan, S., Kendziora, K., and Zins, J. E. (2008). A comprehensive approach to promoting social, emotional, and academic growth in contemporary schools. In A. Thomas & J. Grimes (eds.), *Best practices in school psychology* (Vol. 4, pp. 1263–78). Bethesda, MD: National Association of School Psychologists.

OSPI. (2005). *School improvement planning process guide.* Retrieved from http://k12.wa.us/StudentAndSchoolSuccess/SchImprovementPlanGuide.aspx.

Parrett, W., and Budge, K. (2009, October). Tough questions for tough times. *Educational Leadership, 67*(2), 22–7. Retrieved from http://www.ascd.org/publications-/educational-leadership/oct09/vol67/num02/Tough-Questions-for-Tough-Times.aspx.

Quint, J., Thompson, S. L., and Bald, M. (2008, October). *Relationships, rigor, and readiness: Strategies for improving high schools.* (Paper presented at a conference of midsize school districts convened by MDRC with The Council of the Great City Schools and The National High School Alliance.) Retrieved from http://files.eric.ed.govfulltext/ED502973.pdf.

Salina, C. (2013, July 29). *Formal leadership and change.* Presentation at the Washington Education Association conference, Marysville, WA.

Schmoker, M. (2006). *Results now: How we can achieve unprecedented improvements in teaching and learning.* Alexandria, VA: ASCD.

Servage, L. (2008). Critical and transformative practices in professional learning communities. *Teacher Education Quarterly, 35*(1), 63–77. Retrieved from http://files.eric.ed.gov/fulltext/EJ810651.pdf.

Shepard, J., Salina, C., Girtz, J., Davenport, N., and Broekhart, E. (2010). Student success: Stories that inform high school change. *Reclaiming Children and Youth, 21*(2), 48–53.

Shields, P., and Rangarjan, N. (2013). *A playbook for research methods: Integrating conceptual frameworks and project management.* Stillwater, OK: New Forums Press.

Shouse, R. (1995). *Academic press and school sense of community: Sources of friction, prospects for synthesis.* Retrieved from http://files.eric.ed.gov/fulltext/ED387868.pdf.

Solution Tree. (2012, February 5). *Rebecca DuFour: 3 big ideas of a PLC* [video file]. Retrieved from http://www.youtube.com/v/7-ErgtGzkhs.

Smith, R., and Lambert, M. (2009). Assume the best. In M. Scherer (ed.), *Supporting the whole child: Reflections on best practices in learning, teaching, and leadership* (part 4). Alexandria, VA: ASCD.

Stein, M. K., and Wang, M. C. (1988). Teacher development and school improvement: The process of teacher change. *Teaching and Teacher Education, 4*(2), 171–87.

Steiner, L. M., Ayscue Hassel, E., and Hassel, B. (2008, June). *School turnaround leaders: Competencies for success.* Retrieved from http://www.publicimpact.com/publications/Turnaround_Leader_Competencies.pdf.

Spitzer, R. (2000). Educating in the Catholic tradition. *Catholic Education Resource Center.* Retrieved from http://catholiceducation.org/articles/education/ed0108.html.

Tschannen-Moran, M., and Woolfolk Hoy, A. (2001). Teacher efficacy: Capturing an elusive construct. *Teaching and Teacher Education, 17,* 783–805. Retrieved from http://wps.ablongman.com/wps/media/objects/2347/2404137/Megan_Anita.pdf.

Tschannen-Moran, M., Woolfolk Hoy, A., and Hoy, W. K. (1998). Teacher efficacy: Its meaning and measure. *Review of Educational Research, 68*(2), 202–48.

Wells, G. (1999). *Dialogic inquiry: Towards a sociocultural practice and theory of education.* Cambridge, England: Cambridge University Press.

Zand, D. E. (1997). *The leadership triad: Knowledge, trust, and power.* New York, NY: Oxford University Press.

Index